ONE CITY

ETHAN NICHTERN

ONE CITY

A DECLARATION OF INTERDEPENDENCE

WISDOM PUBLICATIONS • BOSTON

Wisdom Publications
199 Elm Street
Somerville MA 02144 USA
www.wisdompubs.org

Library of Congress Cataloging-in-Publication Data
Nichtern, Ethan.
  One city : a declaration of interdependence / by Ethan Nichtern.
    p. cm.
  Includes index.
  ISBN 0-86171-516-0 (pbk. : alk. paper)
  1. Buddhism--Social aspects. 2. Pratityasamutpada. I. Title.
  BQ4570.S6N53 2007
  294.3'37--dc22
                                    2007014693
11 10 09 08 07
5   4   3   2   1

Cover design by Pema Studios. Interior design by Dede Cummings.
Set in Johanna 11.5/15.5.

Wisdom Publications' books are printed on acid-free paper
and meet the guidelines for permanence and durability of
the Production Guidelines for Book Longevity of the Coun-
cil on Library Resources.

Printed in the United States of America

This book was produced with environmental mindfulness. We
have elected to print this title on 50% PCW recycled paper. As
a result, we have saved the following resources: 44 trees, 30 million
BTUs of energy, 3,828 lbs. of greenhouse gases, 15,890 gallons of
water, and 2,041 lbs. of solid waste. For more information, please
visit our website, www.wisdompubs.org

FOR DR. KING AND TRUNGPA RINPOCHE,

WHO TOOK SOULFUL, BOUNDING LEAPS

TO PUT HUMANS IN TOUCH

WITH THE TWO MOST IMPORTANT TRUTHS:

INTERDEPENDENCE AND BASIC GOODNESS

CONTENTS

CONTENTS

PROLOGUE:
A DAY IN THE LIFE

I WAKE UP IN MY APARTMENT IN BROOKLYN. I slap the snooze button on an alarm clock made in the Philippines. For a few minutes I lie on a bed manufactured in New Jersey, on sheets woven in Mexico, under a blanket from India, reluctantly gathering the mental energy necessary to rise and face another day in NYC. With a deep breath I get out of bed and make coffee with a French press, the way my mother taught me. I grind coffee beans grown on a Puerto Rican plantation. I boil water that comes from a number of reservoirs in upstate New York. This water has pulsed through an intricate web of ducts and unseen pipes that some forgotten engineers constructed decades ago, so that the tens of millions of people in the metropolitan area can stay alive for yet another day. When the coffee is ready, I pour it into a mug manufactured in China that says "Don't Mess With Texas." I add the requisite milk that a few weeks ago pooled inside the udders of cows on a huge industrial farm in Pennsylvania.

Right now, though, I'm not thinking of any of these places, or the people and animals in them. I am concentrating, with the single-mindedness of a junkie, on the familiar taste of coffee.

I brush my teeth and shower—using a toothbrush from Massachusetts, soap from Mexico, shampoo from Ohio, toilet paper from Wisconsin, and a towel from Georgia (the state, not the country). I take asthma medicine manufactured in England. Then I put on my clothes: boxers made in Bangladesh, a T-shirt from Turkmenistan (seriously), pants from Nicaragua, an overshirt from Vietnam, socks from China, a hooded sweatshirt also from China, and a watch with parts from Korea and Taiwan that were assembled in China. All of these things arrived in my apartment thanks to the archaic energy of petroleum.

Not once do I imagine what the people look like who made these clothes. Not once do I consider the long pathways these items had to travel just to be finally stamped with the hidden mental label: "mine."

I sit down to do my morning meditation practice. I settle my mind and gather myself back from a million fantasies and alternate realities, consistently trying to return to the immediacy of the present moment. The practice is incredibly helpful for my sanity, but I didn't invent it. I sometimes forget that my ability to do this practice—to understand my mind at all—depends on the invisible kindness of every teacher I have ever had. In this moment I fail to reflect on the wise, eccentric, and creative geniuses who have collectively helped knit together my own sense of identity. Spacing out, I fall into the trap of thinking I somehow arrived here and now without the guidance of others.

I get up from meditation and put on shoes (made in China). I grab the things I will need for the day (many of which also come from China) and put them into my bag (again, China). I do not notice the irony: for a practitioner of a tradition that has its origins in Tibet, I own a ridiculous amount of stuff from China. But how could I see the irony in this fact? I'm not paying any attention to it.

At this point, I haven't left my apartment. Nonetheless, I have already made contact with and relied upon most of the inhabitants of planet Earth, past and present. I have already made choices that affect all of the inhabitants of planet Earth, present and future. Other than a sleepy grunt to my roommate on the way into the bathroom, I haven't acknowledged contact with anyone or anything at all.

I step out of my building. The day is sunny and bright. I remember to take some time this morning to appreciate the fleeting sunshine. I stand still for a long moment on the front stoop. At least I believe I'm standing still. Actually, the concrete on which my feet seem so firmly planted rotates on its axis at a speed of more than one thousand miles an hour. The borough of Brooklyn hurdles around the sun, ninety-three million miles away, like a tether-ball, at a speed of sixty-seven thousand miles an hour. Meanwhile, within my body, two million dynamic biological operations involving millions of other microbial beings are occurring every second, just so that I can stay alive and falsely believe that I am standing still. I am not still, in any way, shape, or form.

The people on the street in my neighborhood are mostly speaking Spanish, and their families originate from the Dominican Republic, Ecuador, Mexico, Colombia, Guatemala, Venezuela, and Puerto Rico. Like a true New Yorker—wearing anonymity as a badge of honor—I don't acknowledge any of them as we pass each other.

On the way to the subway I see that I have a new message on my cell phone. I dial my voicemail, and the satellite that orbits miles overhead bounces digital information back into my ear. I hear the reconstructed echo of my girlfriend's voice telling me her period is late. *Very.*

I almost knock over a woman on the way down the crowded subway steps. How did all these people get in *My Way?* Hearing the violin-screech of the rush-hour train, I neglect to apologize. I barely make it onboard. The conductor makes a typical post-9/11 announcement about keeping an eye out for suspicious packages. On the crowded car, people are speaking a dozen dialects and languages. The voices stitch themselves into one patchwork patois in the background of my awareness: the dialect of English as it can only be spoken by teenagers in New York City, Spanish, Spanglish, Mandarin, Polish, Japanese, Portuguese, and Haitian French. But I don't pay attention to the symphony of voices. I am only hearing the repetitive thought skipping through my mind like a scratched CD: "*I don't wanna be a daddy!*"

I get off the train and walk upstairs to the street, emerging from the subterranean depths. I find myself in the heart of that island of concrete and humanity that functions as one gargantuan being called Manhattan. There are nine million human bodies on this island during work hours of any given weekday. I am now fully hooked in to the elaborate web of the city, with no specific center and no defined edge. It is a four-dimensional fabric of streets, sidewalks, pipes, tunnels, bricks, steel, glass, graffiti, stores, galleries, parks, homes, relationships, interests, communities, scenes, systems, dreams, intentions, histories, hearts, and minds. And despite all the diverse systems, those amnesiac minds keep forgetting a simple fact: it is still One City.

In many ways, a city responds to events just as the complex systems within an organism respond. Transit strike or power outage, terrorist attack, just one delayed subway on one single train line, and the city will have to reshape itself into a new momentary entity. Within this system, if someone should happen to smile at me—even by accident—I might smile to the rest of the world for hours, spreading warmth along the sidewalk like a lip-curling virus. If I bark at people mindlessly, they might infect twenty other innocent bystanders with their frustration before they even make it to lunch. This is the real Internet—the organic network that transcends cyberspace—and we're all connected, to it and through it.

In the morning I meet one-on-one with a few friends who study meditation with me. It is impossible to talk about the practice of meditation without talking about life, so life is what we end up discussing. One friend asks me questions about the Tibetan Buddhist teachings on what supposedly happens to a person's mind at the time of death. She's only thirty and seems healthy; why is she asking me these questions with so much stress in her voice? I tell her I haven't studied those teachings very thoroughly, so I'm not sure I can tell her what she wants to know. She tells me her heart stopped beating for five minutes when she overdosed on heroin six months ago in Seattle. So now I find myself connected to a drug dealer in

British Columbia I will never meet. At the moment I don't want to meet him. Yet in some small way, he is now a part of my life, too.

Lunch is at my favorite falafel place. The men inside, from Morocco, are speaking to each other in Arabic, but they also speak French and English. I hand the man behind the counter a five-dollar bill, which may have been in the hands of a trucker in South Dakota three days ago. I neglect to thank them for taking the time to make my food, assuming the little green piece of paper I hand them automatically covers all debts of gratitude. I chomp into the falafel like an animal, forgetting that I am one of the fortunate few people on Earth who can easily afford this four-dollar luxury.

After I eat, I flip open my laptop. I find a wireless signal. Now tentacled connections vibrate through the atmosphere as I come into contact with even more people—maybe even *you*. I could Google you and piece together much of your life story. I might be able to deduce the name of someone you have a crush on, too. And you could do the same thing to me. Six degrees of separation was *so* twenty years ago. Now it's two at most. But instead of taking this opportunity to celebrate the bonds between us, I scroll through online news headlines only to become saddened and angered at the state of a world that seems perpetually beyond my reach to affect.

In the afternoon, I meet one of my best friends from childhood for coffee. We've hardly seen each other in the past several years. After college, while I was pursuing Buddhist studies, he joined the Marines. My friend has recently returned from a fifteen-month stint in Iraq, as a First Lieutenant in charge of over forty "men" even younger than he is (he's twenty-six; they are eighteen and nineteen). I ask him what moral lessons war has taught him. Clearly disillusioned, he says that there were no moral lessons to learn, only lessons in survival. Asking him questions, I am struck by the life-and-death decisions he had to make on a daily basis—decisions which I would never, ever be prepared to make.

So now I am connected to the death and destruction in Iraq in a deeper way than I thought. I thought I was connected to the war only by a government that earned my disagreement on almost every issue. I thought I was connected to Iraq by vague headlines scrolling across the bottom of CNN screens, the stoic font of those three little words so vague that they forfeited their power to describe anything at all: "War on Terror." I used to think I was connected to Iraq by the catchy signs that friends and I made for all the protests we attended against the war—the brilliant signs demonstrating that even if we were powerless to stop the war, at least we could be much wittier than the people who started it. But now I am connected to it by my old friend.

A sudden recollection of the two of us hits me: we're seventeen, standing on the tar rooftop of my mother's apartment building, drinking malt liquor, meditating on the 360-degree spectacle of the city's skyline. We're talking about the world as a place of undiscovered destinations and fantasizing about all the girls who are not fantasizing about us.

Snapping back, I am now enmeshed in a war I hate by a dear friend who has been transformed into a seasoned veteran. He's risked his life, watched friends die, and ordered the deaths of others, believing (at least in some small way) that it was for my benefit for him to do these things. I definitely can't fit *all of that* onto one of my protest signs. And it's way too profound and not nearly newsworthy enough for CNN to scroll during a broadcast.

In the evening I teach a class on Buddhist philosophy. I'm overwhelmed by the day. I speak in Buddhist clichés about meditation and why it's a good thing to do. I *hate* when teachers speak to me in that mechanical way that doesn't feel like they are offering any personal experience of the subject at hand. I also forget to ask the names of the students in the class, which is another thing I hate when teachers do.

When I get home, I call my girlfriend: she got her period. My sigh of relief is silent but huge. Of course, I forget to ask her how her day went. I hang up before I even remember to ask her how she's feeling about everything.

Finally exhausted, I crawl under my blanket for a few hours, to escape the world, to find some way to disconnect before tomorrow comes all too soon. But my blanket's label is tickling my nose, nagging at me, offering one final reminder, if I would only take it: I am staying warm tonight only because of the kindness of those men, women, and children in the factory in India, and also the people who work for the shipping company that transported the blanket overseas, and the CEO of the oil company which sold the gas, and the people who paid me a salary so that I could buy the blanket, and on and on and on . . .

PART ONE:
THE REAL
INTERNET

It really boils down to this: that all life is interrelated. We are all caught in an inescapable network of mutuality, tied together into a single garment of destiny. Whatever affects one directly, affects all indirectly. We are made to live together because of the interrelated structure of reality . . . Before you finish eating breakfast in the morning, you've depended on more than half the world. This is the way our universe is structured, this is its interrelated quality. We aren't going to have peace on Earth until we recognize the basic fact of the interrelated structure of all reality.

DR. MARTIN LUTHER KING, JR.

CHAPTER 1:
THE REAL INTERNET

No one is at the center, but each is her own center.

MARGE PIERCY

SOME PARENTS SEND THEIR KIDS TO STUDY painting after school; others to soccer or little league. My mother convinced me to take my first meditation class when I was ten. It was a class just for kids. I remember the girl in front of me complaining to the teacher that I was breathing too loud. The meditation itself was mostly boring and unadorned, a brick wall in a dead-end alley. But I remember having two significant realizations—micro-epiphanies that pierced the boredom of sitting still:

[1] The way my mind went all over the place—projecting whatever fantasy or nightmare it wanted—reminded me of playing a gigantic video game; and

[2] What I thought was happening and what was actually going on when I looked closer were not always

identical. In fact, they usually were not. Sometimes my ideas and reality resided light years apart from each other.

I shrugged away these insights, the way a kid discards all the random scraps of info that his mind can't quite collate into knowledge. Later, as a young teenager, I rebelled against my parents' Buddhist tradition as much as I could. Like every other adolescent, I was looking for something real and meaningful in a world of bland routines and arbitrary rules—constructs that kept being shoved in our face and labeled as absolute truths.

I couldn't meditate just to make my parents happy. I pushed away from their ex-hippie, New-Age group called "Buddhism" in search of a definitive truth that I could claim as mine. In the meantime, I found more meaning in exploring the vibrant, eclectic landscape of New York City youth than I ever found sitting cross-legged in front of a shrine. Every time my parents would invite me to practice meditation with them, all I could do was look at the shrine and think: "Yeah, I'm breathing. That's your big fuckin' realization, my man? *Breathing?* Good for you, Siddhartha." But like most well-intentioned rebellions, mine failed miserably. I tried everything I could think of to escape, and I still couldn't get away from one thing: my own mind.

Like some philosophical aikido or jiujitsu, Buddhist teachings used the force of my own rebellion against me. They used my own cynicism as the momentum with which to bring me careening back to the path of examining myself. They allowed so much room for intelligent questioning that there was ultimately no machine left to rage against. Eventually it became clear that my meditation practice was just incredibly helpful to making it through life without caving in to anxiety and depression. By the end of high school I was meditating regularly. I could feel myself becoming more confident, getting more in touch with myself—especially those dark and murky parts of my mind that I'd usually rather be left alone.

EVENTUALLY, meditation leads us beyond an examination of our own mind and into an exploration of the world we live in. So often I hear people—myself included—fall into a seductive trap in the way we discuss events and culture: we speak of the contemporary world as if we're witnessing the unfolding of someone else's nightmare. It's an interesting nightmare—equipped with many compelling characters and melodramatic scenarios—but we feel personally disconnected from the plot. A lot of the time, we interact with our experience as if THE WORLD were reality TV, as if we were staring at our own society on some fifty-inch high-definition plasma screen.

THE WORLD is fun to watch sometimes, but most of the time, it is straight-up depressing. Sometimes we tune in to THE WORLD just for its shock value. We get some kind of twisted kick out of how god-awful it all is—the frenzy of tsunamis and global warming–induced hurricanes, genocides, ludicrous profit-motives, and misguided political ambitions. And in those rare moments when we actually take the time to look at what's going on and feel some real empathy with the human characters in THE WORLD, of course our hearts crumble.

Most of us wish THE WORLD were different, kinder, more creative, more balanced somehow. But we can't take any personal blame for creating this world; it is out of our hands—we're just watching it on the screen. We inherited it from people who screwed everything up, who inherited it from people who fucked everything up before them, an infinite regress, an endless human pedigree of stupidity. So we sink back into couches, looking for some new and improved remote control with which to change our mental channel, trying to forget what we've seen on the screen. If all else fails, maybe we can find a deep hole to crawl into and write an eye-opening manifesto, like the heroes of Ralph Ellison or Dostoevsky.

THIS IS WHERE THE BUDDHA BECOMES IMPORTANT as a historical figure. The Buddha was no Underground Man. It is sometimes said that the Buddha was a prince, but the important thing is that he was a child of privilege. A group of teenagers studying meditation told me that the Buddha sounded like a rich kid from the Upper East Side of Manhattan. Through the decades of his teens and twenties, he became increasingly disillusioned with the society he lived in, particularly with his father's troubling assumption that he who dies with the highest status will be proclaimed the winner of the Game of Life. The young prince became increasingly convinced that bling does not equal happiness. And so, at the age of twenty-nine, he left his family in search of a new way of being a human being.

He did not withdraw from the world because he'd given up on it. His disillusionment with the society in which he grew up was matched by a great hopefulness for both personal and societal transformation. The Buddha (temporarily) withdrew from the world so he could understand it more fully, to learn to transform self-absorption and self-loathing into compassionate action. Meditation was his main method for affecting this transformation. From his period of withdrawal and reflection, he came to understand that he was inextricably a part of the world, and that the world was a part of him. "Retreat" from life had never really been an option. His own personal identity was hopelessly, brilliantly entwined with the state of the world in which he lived. In short, what he realized is that everything is interdependent.

NOTHING EXISTS IN A VACUUM. What we see as separate (and often opposing) entities really come into being precisely through their dependence on each other. If you took a moment to reflect on all of the influences, conditions, and forces that brought this little book into your hands right now (the teachers and parents who taught you to read, the friend who recommended the book to you or the stock clerk in the bookstore, the writer's influences, the paper mill that made the paper, the publisher), you would find infinite contributing causes that do not, could not, exist separately of each other. You would also find that you are not just holding several (recycled) sheets of paper but are right now connecting to a much larger number of people than you would ever account for in your personal acquaintances.

Likewise, if you traced out the effects of one of your simple daily actions, you might be overwhelmed by the complexity of all the ripples you create. If you buy bottled water instead of using a refillable water bottle, you are raising the CO_2 level above Greenland and affecting the livelihoods of oil workers in Nigeria. How many of us have the patience and awareness to contemplate these effects without either freezing up in guilt or rolling our eyes in apathy when we grab that Poland Spring at our corner deli?

The Buddha also realized another aspect of interdependence. Interdependence doesn't only mean that conditions and events in the world exist inseparably from one and other—like the link between a half-liter plastic bottle, oil, and the environment. It also means that the mindsets of individuals and the society that those individuals co-produce are likewise inextricably connected. The logic of this relationship is almost painfully obvious: our society has manifested in its present form because the people who comprise it—knowingly or not—collectively acted to make it this way. So where do those actions come from? They spring from the thoughts, habits, and conditioned beliefs of the many individuals who create our society. Not only is it important for us to examine our actions in the world, but we also need an ongoing method for examining the thoughts, habits, and belief structures from which those actions unfold. This is why meditation is crucial.

When the Buddha saw the truth of interdependence, he didn't just have a blinking glimpse of this realization that boggles the mind and unravels our isolationist tendencies. It is said that his mind could simply rest in that awareness, fully connected to the *real* Internet, never losing the signal. He no longer sought any escape from the worldwide web of causes, conditions, beings, and interactions that constituted himself and all reality. He wasn't afraid of the profound implications of that knowledge; his heart wasn't overwhelmed by the experience. Seeing interdependence caused him to fall *deeply and hopelessly in love with reality*. From this deep connection, compassion exploded with the pure force of nuclear fusion.

THE BUDDHA SAID there were eighty-four thousand distinct ways to discuss his own teachings—but that was a conservative estimate. This is why there are now books on Buddhism and art, Buddhism and business, *Buddhism for Dummies*, Buddhist cookbooks, even Buddhist golf books. I haven't checked, but there might even be a book about Buddhist teachings for your toy poodle. At its core, the tradition is ridiculously simple. As my main Buddhist teacher Sakyong Mipham Rinpoche says, it's about learning *how to love*—period.

This truth makes Buddhism no different from any other spiritual impulse or any other wisdom tradition that has ever existed. This may be disappointing for those of us who always want to be one step ahead of everyone else, living on the razor's edge of hipster trends. And it will definitely cause a problem if we want to claim personal possession of the most *avant-garde* philosophies. In some ways, Buddhism is about as retro as you can get. I saw a great T-shirt the other day that said "EVERYTHING YOU LIKE, I LIKED FIVE YEARS AGO." Another version of this shirt might say: "Every insight you have, the Buddha had twenty-six hundred years ago." Maybe we should stop worrying so much about being original.

In order to really understand and embody love, we have to understand interdependence. Interdependence doesn't just describe issues of global importance; it occurs on every level of our experience simultaneously, from the construction of our own personal identity all the way up to the ungraspable complexities of human society.

Sometimes when we quest for a hidden spiritual truth, we miss what's right in front of us. Fumbling blindly for the mystical, we miss what is holy within the mundane event of walking down a city street. Interdependence only *seems* like

9

a profound truth because we don't recognize it 99% of the time. While we're lost in the thought-bubbles of "then and there," interdependence always, already resides *here and now*. There is nothing mystical about this truth. When we encounter it, it strikes us like a big fat "Duh!"

Buddhist teachings can only be found in daily life—and they're there whether we notice them or not. They don't descend from some heavenly realm or operate on some rainbow plane of consciousness. And "a day in the life"—your life—is the only place you can experience truth, especially the truth of interdependence. You've probably had much more exciting days than the one I recounted in the prologue. But even the most boring day serves as a perfect reminder that no part of our lives occurs in the vacuum of outer space.

For those of us who live in big cities, the fine strands of the webbing that holds us together are extra visible. Sometimes our connection to other people is claustrophobically apparent, right smack in front of our face when those subway doors slide open at rush hour. With the in-your-face nature of city dwelling, a metropolis might surprisingly be ideal for practicing and realizing this truth (though of course, suburbanites and rural folks experience interdependence too). Instead of serving as a constant reminder of interdependence, however, a day of life in a big city is often spent maintaining caustic boundaries, yelling into cell-phones, averting our eyes from each other and holding our noses.

Millions of people choose to live packed like sardines in tins (which we call "studio apartments"), separated by only a few feet and thin plaster walls. And the reason we've chosen to live like this? Because human beings are simply not self-sufficient. We rely on each other for work, education, sustenance, friendship, art, culture, community, and love. Yet so much of the time we scurry from place to place, task to task, moment to moment, craving isolation and feigning anonymity. This is the paradox of contemporary living.

THE IDEA OF INTERDEPENDENCE is not unique to Buddhist thought at all. There is a growing movement calling for more holistic and integrated ways of examining many global issues. People are declaring interdependence all over the place, in a variety of fields of inquiry. Many are trying to find ways to look at twenty-first-century issues without compartmentalizing problems, without analyzing them as if they existed apart from each other in separate, mutually exclusive spheres. These trends are most evident in areas like globalization, conflict resolution, and climate study. Likewise, narrative and visual arts are increasingly addressing the nature of expression from more interwoven perspectives. Again, there isn't much about Buddhism that's really "Buddhist." After all, *buddha* is just a Sanskrit word that means "someone who is awake." A Buddhist is someone who's trying to wake up to the real conditions of her or his life. That's all.

What makes Buddhism relevant to the twenty-first century is that—unlike many theories of global interdependence—the study of Buddhism begins in each individual's heart and mind. On this level, love isn't a vague, Hallmark-card idea. The kind of love that deeply understands interdependence involves precision, rigor, and a method of in-depth training. Love requires learning to look ourselves in the mirror, and learning to look other people in the eye. Buddhism, in turn, asks us to pause and look at even the subtlest causal connections and take our appreciation of them to greater depths. Meditation allows us to explore the building blocks that create our personal identities. Meditation forces us to not look at the world as a vague entity; it asks us to constantly examine our own mind's role in the unfolding of each event. It directs us to witness the interdependence between our own habitual tendencies and the manifestation of the communities in which we live.

A lot of theories about how to make a positive difference in this world only examine and critique our collective issues on the macro or societal level. So often we forget to consistently examine ourselves as the very individuals who make up the systems of thought, expression, and action in which we collectively engage. For example, I may have truly wonderful ideas about the pitfalls of American consumerism, but have I taken the time necessary to familiarize myself with the mechanism by which my own mind craves things, moment by moment? As I discuss the nature of American consumerism, I should also probably become deeply familiar with the vacuum cleaner that is my own consumerism.

Buddhism's contribution to the study of interdependence starts with individuals trying to understand what makes our minds tick—why we want what we want, fear what we fear, act how we act, do what we do. From there, we can initiate a discussion about how our world works. And once we gain some insight into the projector (our minds) and the projection (the world), we can begin to transform our personal projectors and that collective projection, in small ways and big ones. Who knows what this world might look like if we transformed it? It might look a little bit different. Or maybe, we might just look at it a little differently. Either way, understanding the mind is the skeleton key.

CHAPTER 2:
THE INADEQUACY PRINCIPLE

I would like to say, ladies and gentlemen, that you shouldn't be afraid of who you are. That's the first key idea. You shouldn't be afraid of who you are. You should not be afraid of who you are. It's very important for you to realize that.

CHOGYAM TRUNGPA RINPOCHE

MY RIDE DROPS ME OFF IN TIMES SQUARE. It's Super Bowl Sunday, just before game time. My feet touch the familiar sidewalk: I'm in the strangest spot in that strange human realm called America, on the strangest day of the year. Many millions of people are busy planning parties to celebrate a four-hour long commercial masquerading as a football game. I wonder if this is how a Martian would feel touching down on Earth. None of this should be unfamiliar. I'm an American and the Super Bowl is America's Ritual. Times Square is the Crossroads of the World. But it feels eons away from where I've just been.

A few hours ago I was at the end of a month-long meditation retreat in Northern Vermont. The hills were blinding white with untrammeled snow (in NYC the snow turns to grey paste before it even hits the concrete). The land was calm, as if the snow had turned down the volume on everything. I was hugging other students goodbye, exchanging phone numbers and email addresses, preparing to return to the Real World. We'd been with each other for the past month, meditating and studying texts—some ancient, some contemporary—about mindfulness and compassion. We were learning how to avoid sleepwalking through life. That was where I was this morning.

Now I am straight off the highway, catapulted back into the Real World. Massive billboards hang over crowds of tourists. Jumbotrons cover the space like haphazard video wallpaper. There's nowhere to rest my eyes; nothing remains still long enough to be examined. The whole world is on fire with façades. The air is electrified, humming with low bass, thick and neon. The Pop Diva of the Moment is fifteen feet tall and a Pepsi logo is tattooed to her breasts. After about five seconds, the Diva's breasts are tattooed to the inside of my eyelids, and I can almost taste the Pepsi. Cars, cell-phones, clothes, TV shows, women, sex, ideas, nostalgia, well-being, and spirituality—all for perpetual sale. MSNBC news, on the big Panasonic screen, comes across as just another ad. No longer a public space, this is a huge film set—Walt Disney meets *Blade Runner* with a tab of acid thrown in. I can't even tell what product is being advertised on most of the billboards, but the message about what I am supposed to do is still loud and clear: *WANT. KEEP WANTING. WANT A LOT.*

Welcome home, I think.

LATER ON IN THE DAY, I'm standing in front of a magazine rack, contemplating the massive shrine of glossy images. The women on about seventy magazine covers are returning my stare, and so are a few men. Those who happen to be hot right now appear on more than one cover.

Still, the elements of all the covers are amazingly uniform—similar backdrops, similar outfits, similar hairstyles, similar hints of elite lifestyles, similar looks on their airbrushed faces. They don't appear to have to struggle at all to be so wonderful (unless "struggle" happens to be chic this month). The text that frames their faces is about superquick steps to self-improvement, usually three or five but no more than ten (who has the attention span to follow twenty steps?). The subtext behind their bodies is about sex and success, and you are either supposed to want to *be* it or want to *get* it.

WHILE I'M LOCKED IN A STARING CONTEST with Tom Cruise, it begins to dawn on me that I was doing something very important during that month-long meditation program. I was not escaping from the world of Times Squares and magazine racks. Instead, I was taking the time necessary to get more in touch with My Own Private Times Square.

My Own Private Times Square is that inner realm where all the ads are placed by subsidiary companies of the imaginary MegaTransNational Corporation called Hopes and Fears, Inc. This particular branch of the corporation—called ME—was founded in 1978. But the corporation itself has been around much longer than that, operating under different names and charters.

The subsidiary companies of this MegaTransNational Corporation rent chemical space inside my mind to sell me their various lines of lifestyle products. They plaster massive thought-billboards and bombard me with 24/7 messages, until I get their jingles stuck in my head like the lyrics of a Madonna song. There has been a constant thought-ad campaign running since I was a little kid, though I like to pretend that it has become more sophisticated as I've matured.

The basic message has always been the same: "You are not enough." The longer version goes like this: "Face it— you were never one of the cool kids. In fact, you've never even been close to cool. For this transgression, you shall forever remain unworthy of the blessings in your life. You are inadequate in ways you can't even describe or pinpoint. But if you do THIS, if you get THAT, if you believe the other thing, then you might, maybe, possibly, be okay (but only for a little while)." I've become the worst kind of consumer— a consumer of unmeetable expectations. My inner Times Square makes the outer Times Square look like a playpen in comparison. So much time in life has been lost chasing the morphing ghosts of Cool, when I could've been learning how to be Kind.

ALONG WITH THE HUNDREDS OF OTHER IMAGES of women (and men) that we see every day on TV and movie screens, the faces on the magazine rack form one vague but cohesive personality, one superhuman ideal that shifts slightly (and profitably) with whatever style is seasonally declared. This superhuman figure embodies a perfection of sexuality and a fulfillment of lifestyle. Call her MegaGirl—a superhero whose superpower isn't anything specific. She doesn't really do anything, like fly a thousand miles an hour, solve world hunger, or spit raging balls of fire. It's not about what she does. It's about what she has. She's got IT. Just don't ask what IT is, because you won't get a straight answer from anyone. IT is a shadow; IT is a whisper; IT is something *we* could never possess, unless we buy into the image and its accessories. Even then, we don't get to own IT. We are only leasing IT for as long as IT lasts—which is not long at all.

MegaGirl is the bane of the existence of every actual girl and woman I have ever known or loved. No matter how ultrafeminist and revolutionary they might be, no matter how secure in themselves they are, they are nagged constantly by MegaGirl's long, dark shadow. Her ominous voice of judgment lurks in the back of their skulls. Even those women who revolt against MegaGirl's oppression, those who've read or written a thousand essays denouncing the objectification of women in all its subtle forms—all of them live with MegaGirl. She is a psychic force to be reckoned with on that rack. And even the women I know who come close to actually attaining her unattainable image always have to worry about their own objectification, and the insecurity that comes from the fear of losing their tentative status as MegaGirls themselves.

MegaGirl (along with her partner MegaGuy) is also the bane of the existence of every guy I have ever known. They don't feel the pressure of trying to *become* MegaGirl. Instead, they feel the immense pressure of doing what it takes, saying what it takes, buying what it takes, and becoming *who* it takes to be *with* MegaGirl. And what we want to do when we're with her is also lying just below the surface of her gloss.

Only MegaGuy gets to be with MegaGirl, right? That's the way the story is always told (in the heterosexual version, at least—and the homosexual version leads to a similar conclusion).

The power of these comic-book ideals is derived entirely from a state of mind that fails to examine itself carefully. It relies on witnessing moments of assumed perfection out of the corners of our eyes, remaining passive observers to their effects. Without self-reflection, each and every time we become a passive observer of the media we experience, we soak up negative messages like sponges, even when we're already somewhat aware of the message's aggressive presence. We rarely take the opportunity to reflect on how our ideals of perfection are and have been internally constructed, engrained, and perpetuated since time immemorial. But if we really took a few moments to examine how we're defining our version of perfection, it's pretty easy to see that the *ideal doesn't exist*. This is not to say that it doesn't exist in the clichéd Buddhist way of saying "there is no self." It's simpler than that: the "woman" or "man" we see on the cover of a magazine isn't even a real person.

Think about what it takes for that image to come before our eyes on the cover of a magazine, a billboard or flatscreen. By the time we see the group of images on the rack, the group of pixels on the TV or the group of façades on billboards, there is very little in the processed images and tightly arranged moments that corresponds to anything we could call a "real" person. Sure, a real person did walk into the photo shoot, but if the image we see is actually one of several hundred of each model taken in that shoot, and then that one image is carefully edited, modified and retouched, then where is the "person" in the image? Where is the human life, the pulse of heartbeat and murmur of breath under that façade? And even if we already know it's just a façade, somehow we still can't help but bow down, prostrate to it anyway.

AN IMAGE FREEZES and crystallizes one or a few carefully chosen moments—hooked and netted like dead fish from the vast sea of moments that make up an actual human life. The chosen moment is framed, manicured, and manipulated to cleverly remove it from the dynamic and awkward context in which the true flow of life takes place.

What meditation shows us is that we have a strong tendency to do the exact same thing with our own mental experience. We constantly edit, reshape, and crop our own thoughts. We escape into rehashed moments of fantasy, falsified memories of what could or might have been that are more mentally photogenic than this present moment.

Whether an advertiser is trying to sell it to us or we are "selling" it to ourselves within our own thought process, the perception of any awkward moments must be removed. After all, our lives are already packed with awkward moments, and we aren't trying to "buy" any more of them. Real life is not that mirror face we try to superimpose onto our own when we stare at our reflection. Real life is embarrassing. Real life is doing stupid things we hope no one saw. Real life is spinach stuck in our teeth for six hours.

These framed and edited moments that surround and permeate us have a tremendous amount of power, much like the self-images that constantly flicker through our minds. The power comes from the impulse—so difficult to avoid—to measure our experience against an ideal that's not based on the raw and uncut nature of actual experience. Instead of finding beauty and meaning within the messy present moment, we tell each other (and ourselves) to find beauty and meaning in moments that literally *never existed*, except as amplified echoes and high-definition mirages. And when we hold our own "imperfect" experience up to vague ideals and then judge ourselves in relationship to the ideal, there's only one way we could possibly feel about the comparison: *Inadequate. Totally Fucking Inadequate.*

IT'S POPULAR to equate Buddhism with the idea that "life is suffering." Some very simplistic takes of the four noble truths (the first formal teaching that the Buddha gave which addresses the nature of suffering) do make it seem like all Buddhism has to offer is the cold, hard fact of suffering and turmoil. There's a rap by Nas that has the chorus: "Life's a bitch and then you die / that's why we get high." This isn't exactly what Buddhism means when it refers to suffering. Suffering is not the nature of our experience; it arises from *misunderstanding* our experience. This misunderstanding is what we have to face.

The judgment of our own being relative to unattainable perfection—and the feeling of inadequacy that *must result* from the false comparison—isn't at all new to the twenty-first century. It is the most general formula for confusion, on a very basic level of human consciousness. The discussion of suffering gets a lot more complicated than this simple way of looking at it. However, at its root, suffering occurs when whatever we have—whatever we are—is assumed to be *not right*—not enough, too much, just somehow off.

In our misguided attempts to solve this problem, we create a tremendous amount of turmoil, because we have to acquire or destroy whatever it takes to move toward the constructed ideal and away from the inadequacy of the present moment. Of course, when we actually do get what we were trying to acquire (next-generation gear, the right apartment, lovers who make our friends congratulate us out loud and talk trash about us under their breath, the most profound spiritual truths), and destroy what we were trying to destroy, the problem stays unsolved. It stays unsolved because our constructed ideal is by definition slippery, always changing; and like a chameleon it easily transforms into something new. The ideal is forever a shifting lifestyle and personal identity, always somehow disconnected from the reality of our moment-by-moment experience.

What we thought was IT a very short time ago is not anymore. What we think will get us by right now will soon no longer suffice. What we actually have, here and now, could never be acceptable, because we already have it. So we start the process over again, acquiring, destroying, manipulating, editing, airbrushing, and Photoshopping the moments of our experience, hoping to catch up with that fleeting ideal in our minds.

Some great thinkers (like Naomi Klein) have written about how companies don't sell items anymore, they sell the perception of entire perfected lifestyles, in which a whole way of being/consuming in the world is implied and promised. The trick is that within a simple ad for one product, you can get someone to feel simultaneously incomplete without hundreds of other similar lifestyle products. A suburban teenager buys a pair of shoes because he thinks they make him look and feel more urban, more hardcore, more concrete and real. He wants the urban feeling; he's not really in it for that specific pair of shoes. So any commercial that makes him feel more hardcore becomes an ad for shoes that fit that lifestyle perception in his mind, whether or not it's a shoe ad. What might nominally be a Lexus commercial also becomes a commercial for everything else that might go with the Lexus lifestyle—the house in a gated community, the intelligent trophy-wife or the heroic (but sensitive) husband, the ivy-league dream realized. I might buy an expensive hooded sweatshirt instead of a Lexus, but I've bought into the Inadequacy Principle either way.

The mental impulse to chase an image of perfection is what keeps us coming back for another serving of inadequacy. It's like a bad remake of an old movie that we didn't even like the first time. The characters, the setting, the dialogue, and the plot are sort of new each time the script gets reworked, but the whole process is, more-or-less, circular and repetitive. That's the definition of *samsara*, the déjà vu cycle of confused and destructive habits.

Of course, our modern culture of manufactured desires only intensifies the feeling of this inadequacy. We are utterly bombarded 24/7/365 by advertising meant to show us something we don't have (but could rent pieces of, because, after all we're *worth* it!). The more bombarded we get, the less space we have to examine how our ideas of perfection are manufactured at the mental source, how they fountain out of our own insecure self-image.

In the age of advertising, even the idea of "living in the moment" is taken out of context. Rather than serving as a means of appreciating what we already have, "living in the moment" is the advertiser's slogan for justifying indulgence and compulsiveness. Don't worry what your credit-card statement will look like next month—*live in the moment, live richly!*

When we have no way to rest with the present moment, its ups, downs, and scattered vicissitudes, we become rampant consumers of our own experience and colonizers of our own minds. We start using our own natural resources to impose oppressive ideas of the way we're supposed to be.

This is how I find myself craving the latest iPod when a few years ago a cassette Walkman was more than enough. This is how our thoughts can become a cacophony of all the reasons we hate ourselves (the reasons might change over time, but the cacophony keeps on going). This is why so many people care where that A-list person of the moment eats breakfast. Her imaginary breakfast is a lot less interesting than our own real breakfast, if we actually invested ourselves in tasting it.

THERE ARE CERTAIN TRADITIONAL characteristics that an enlightened person is supposed to possess, certain ways such a person acts and moves through the world. Some are supernatural and ridiculous: for example, it is traditionally said that a Buddha's clothing perpetually levitates four finger-widths above his flesh! But one trait of an enlightened person is truly more superheroic than all the others: A Buddha doesn't act *any differently* whether she is among other people or all by herself. She doesn't put on any façades; she doesn't wish she were someone else; she doesn't say what she thinks other people want her to say; she doesn't worry if other people think she looks all right. She *does* look all right. She *is* all right. She has no affect, zero pretense. Her presence is 100% authentic. And that authenticity makes her an incredibly powerful person. Her inner strength comes from an underlying feeling of *total adequacy*. And this strength radiates out from her to the people around her, as if she were a living billboard blazing this slogan: "You're *great* as you are. *No joke.*" She's not trying to sell an image of herself to anyone—especially not herself. And for this feat, she is, you could say, "*extra*" ordinary.

It sounds great, right? Being completely comfortable in our own transient skin sounds like an *ideal* way to be. For a meditator, there is always that same danger of worshiping this image as yet another ideal, a statuesque, bronzed billboard of a being who has attained that elusive perfection—a Buddha—a being we could never ourselves become. Enlightenment itself becomes another A-list fantasy for C-list people, perpetually distant from where we are. When we fall into this trap, we can't actually become more open, more secure people—and practicing meditation just becomes another way of chasing an image.

"Spirituality" can also just mean constructing and buying into a new lifestyle (not the urban-hip-hop lifestyle, not the starving-artist-hipster lifestyle, not the chic-yuppie-send-my-kids-to-Brown-University-someday lifestyle, but the Buddhist strike-a-lotus-pose lifestyle) marked by consumption of unattainable goals and unrealistic "spiritual" expectations. And we can spend a mountain of money on all the spiritual gear that goes with the Buddhist lifestyle: the retreats, the cushions, the incense, not to mention the yoga mats and endless supply of organic "wellness" products. If the Inadequacy Principle dominates our spiritual path as well, then that path will only serve as a new-and-improved means of feeling the haunting buzz of worthlessness all over again. Repeating some New-Age mantra, or having the "Buddhist accessories" isn't enough. There is no quick fix, no five easy steps to losing our mind's flab.

If meditation has a real usefulness in dealing with the Inadequacy Principle, then it has to actually move us, little-by-little, in the direction of feeling worthy of our life. This doesn't necessarily mean giving up everything we own. That might just be another lifestyle built on the insecure pretense of a false ideal (the self-denying-ascetic lifestyle).

The Buddha, that woman or man who has no pretense in her/his being, can't be just an ideal, much less an idol. This person needs to be human—whether or not the cameras are rolling or flashbulbs are popping.

THE COUNTERARGUMENT is always this: what if something really is missing, what if some quality in you isn't fully developed, and what if there is a way you can develop these qualities further and find new fulfillment? Who doesn't want to make his life better? After all, if there were nothing to train or develop, no goal, then there wouldn't be a reason to do much of anything, least of all engaging in the tedious process of getting to know our minds more thoroughly. If Buddhism is just about blindly accepting what is and never hoping for something better, then maybe it is just another opiate of the masses. (Can you imagine if a friend said to you: "You gotta check out meditation. It's going to do absolutely *nothing* for you!" Not the best way to spread the word about a meditation group . . .)

Of course we want to be better people, to be more creative, productive, and fulfilled in the areas that make us feel alive. But the crux of the matter is what we believe lies at the essential core of our identity. If we think that what we are at the very foundation is originally sinful, fucked-up, confused, untalented, and worthless, then any attempt to develop ourselves is going to run into irreconcilable problems. With this perspective, any self-improvement would be a temporary solution, a sweeping of our dirty little secrets under the proverbial rug. Even the spiritual path would just be some new kind of extreme makeover, whitewashing a thin layer of spiritual presentability on top of the inadequate base of who we truly are. We can put a glossy patina over a rotten interior, but the gloss will always fade; we will never be lastingly satisfied with the "improvements" we've made. We will always crash back to a state of inadequacy, no matter how professional the makeover, no matter how many "steps" have been prescribed to reach a better "us."

On the other hand, if we think the bedrock of our identity, the fundamental basis upon which we'd like to develop ourselves, is actually wise, compassionate, and creative, then the changes we make will be processes of developing this foundation, of making our intelligent core more manifest in our lifestyle. In the end, this would be the only way to make changes that aren't temporary coverings for a deep and underlying self-loathing. And in fact, to engage in any path of well-being or self-development, some small part of us must already believe that we're worth developing.

PRACTICING MEDITATION provides a radical way of dealing with the timeless problem of our conditioned inadequacy. Meditation delivers to us our experience, unplugged. Because the very process of meditation forces us to examine ourselves in a way that we can't retouch and adorn with distractions and expectations as easily, we begin to see how much of our life is wasted in fantasy, daydreams, and vivid, waking nightmares.

Somehow, through meditation, the pursuit of the non-existent ideal becomes less and less meaningful. A meditator begins to witness the fantasy directly, without the movie soundtrack, no logos. Without these adornments to brand the false experience, it's not so impressive. And as we familiarize ourselves with our ideals over and over again, we start to see that the unreality truly does nothing but destabilize our hearts.

The Inadequacy Principle leaves us close-minded, deluded, and disconnected from interdependence. Like ghosts, we're physically here, but we're always wishing we were somewhere else, *someway* else, *someone* else. A life lived in inadequacy gives us CDD (Compassion Deficit Disorder). While we are busy scouring our brains for that perfect identity which we are *not*, the real people we care about are left waiting for us in the real world.

The real world has a potency that the world of idealized images will never touch. In the real world—where interdependence occurs every single moment—we are ourselves. In the real world we are ordinary. And the more ordinary we get, the more *extra*-ordinary we become.

CHAPTER 3:
TOUCHING THE NET

You know the motto:
Stay fluid, even in staccato.

MOS DEF

OUR PERSONAL EXISTENCE occurs on many different levels at once, from micro to macro. Our states of mind are determined within the tiniest details of the random smile to a stranger or that single bite of falafel sandwich. Our life is also constantly affected by the biggest elements of the big picture—the systemic functioning of a country with millions of inhabitants, and a planet with billions. Understanding interdependence is prerequisite for knowing how it all works—not only our own hearts and minds, but also the factors that lead to global conflict and complex international relationships.

Let's now look at five levels of interdependence: the interdependence of the self, interdependence in relationships, interdependence in communities, global or societal interdependence, and universal interdependence. On each level, the truth of interdependence has distinct implications. At the same time, the five levels constantly affect one another, and can ultimately only be separated from each other for the purposes of description and understanding—not in reality. What's more, effects don't only emanate outward, but likewise come full circle back to the source.

A complete understanding of cause and effect must take into account the constant crisscrossing and mutual reverberations of these personal, interpersonal, communal, and global levels of interaction. Therefore a detailed exploration of the topic of interdependence becomes vast, elusive, and hopelessly enmeshed. Ultimately speaking, it is impossible to discuss interdependence on any of these five levels as a free-standing entity, without relationship to the other levels of our interaction. It is never truthful to speak about how you treat your ex as a separate reality from the current state of affairs in Afghanistan. However, because our lives do occur on many levels simultaneously—the personal, the interpersonal, the communal, and the global—it makes sense to divide the discussion of interdependence and examine its manifestations separately.

An architect might learn something new about his design from examining the sketches of the tenth floor of a skyscraper. A real building, however, can never only have a tenth floor without (at least) nine others. Similarly, we can't have a society without having many individuals, yet it is helpful to examine the identities of individuals as distinct (but connected) entities from the society at large.

It is impossible for us as human beings with human minds to get an objective bird's-eye view of interdependence. We may not each be the center of the known universe; the belief that we are is a big part of our problems. However, we are each at the center of our subjective experience; there's no way to get outside of ourselves. So it is with our own selves that awareness of the world starts—there's no other way to look into anything. Accordingly, our investigation of interdependence begins with ourselves and radiates outward from us—into our relationships, communities, and society.

INTERDEPENDENCE OF THE SELF

The first—and maybe most crucial—place we encounter this truth is in the construction of our own personal identity. Our identity is never reducible to any single factor or element. It can't be encapsulated in quick labels like "Progressive," or "Artist," or "African-American," no matter how much we try to pin individuals down. Regardless, we have a deep tendency to put ourselves and others into convenient boxes that can be easily checked off. This tendency makes life simpler and lets us summarize individuals in a way with which we feel comfortable. But the labels never accurately describe anyone, because labels are singular and identity is not.

When I was little, possibly the biggest treat in my life was going to FAO Schwartz, a massive, fancy toy store in New York. The Lego displays caught my eye every time—mammoth sculptures of towering dinosaurs, gargantuan robots, and larger-than-life Lego people. From across the store, the Lego robots looked solid and statuesque—whole, complete, and monolithic. But when I got up close, I could see all the tiny fissures between the individual Lego pieces, and I could see the thousands and thousands of building blocks, all different colors and shapes interlocking, that made up the thing in front of me. That eight-foot tall dinosaur was really a heap of many tiny pieces, perfectly arranged to create the impression of a singular, unchangeable whole.

When we become aware of the myriad building-blocks of our identity, we get new perspective on who and what we are. What we sometimes mistakenly assume to be one mind, one being, one self, one "me," is really a construct comprising many interlocking elements. I am never one thing; I am always many. And the many things that I am are themselves the result of, and connected to, many other things.

So is the mind like a giant Lego dinosaur? Not quite. Obviously, the building blocks of our identity aren't themselves solid brick or plastic; they're liquid, fluid, coasting and morphing to the breakbeat rhythm of impermanence. Our identities are constantly reshaped by the continual introduction of new experiences, influences, and perspectives. If my mind were really like a monolithic statue, then I would like the same music at age twenty-nine that I liked at age nine (Def Leppard doesn't do it for me anymore; Mos Def does). Scientifically speaking, my physical body now contains none of the same physical or chemical matter that it did when I was nine, with the exception of a few cell types that change more slowly (but nonetheless do change).

The interdependence of the self is one way to talk about the Buddhist idea of *egolessness*. To be clear, nobody is claiming that we don't exist, that you and I aren't "real"— though that's a common misunderstanding of this idea. If we didn't exist, it would certainly let us off the hook of responsibility for dealing with interdependence!

Egolessness is the interdependence of the self. So what does that mean? If I say the words "Hudson River," you might recall the river from memory, or at least can infer the general meaning of "Hudson River" from the experience you've had of other rivers. If you've been near the Hudson in New York City, you have a memory of a body of water flowing between the West Side of Manhattan and New Jersey. You might recall the buildings that line each bank, the crystal and concrete towers of Manhattan and the housing complexes of suburban New Jersey. The way the sunlight hits that water at five o'clock on a spring afternoon is unlike anywhere else on Earth. You wouldn't think of the East River or the Mississippi River or the Seine or the Nile, which are different rivers, different beings, distinct bodies with separate—but connected—identities.

If we go look at the Hudson River and really examine it closely, it becomes much more difficult to pin down the exact material that *defines* the Hudson River as such. Is the river defined merely by the water in it? All of the molecules of water we see today are going to be miles downriver tomorrow, replaced by totally different molecules—and totally different pieces of garbage and shoes and toilet seats floating in the water. And then that water, and that garbage, will be part of the Atlantic Ocean. So the Hudson River can't be defined by the specific molecules or objects flowing between the boundaries of New York and New Jersey at this precise moment. Then is the river defined by the banks that outline it, the borders that create its external boundaries? Doesn't it seem problematic to define something solely by the space around it, by the realm of what it is *not*?

What happens if Donald Trump builds new high-rise apartments on the shores and changes the appearance of the riverbanks (and the property values)? Is that still the same Hudson River?

Without awareness, we fall into traps, defining the rivers of our selves either (a) completely in terms of the experiences and mind-state that we identify with right now (the water) or (b) by constantly inferring our identity from that which is other than us, inferring a solid identity in relationship to that which is outside us (the banks of the river). If I want to be known around the world as "the greatest writer of my generation," I might pin my entire identity on my current volume of work. I would also worry incessantly about what other people think of my writing. One bad review means total devastation: my whole being is shredded, no longer worth the paper to which I tried to affix my self-value.

Our identity isn't as solid as we think—but there must still be a continuity of experience. Each time I return, I recognize the Hudson River, no matter how many new buildings Mr. Trump has built up alongside it. In the same way, when I see a picture of myself as a nine-year-old, I know that there is a connection between that kid in the picture and the man in the mirror. Despite all the problems I have in pinning the tail on my lasting SELF, the kid in the photo and the guy in the mirror seem to have the same exact smirk on their faces.

It's good to contemplate all of the forces that have brought us into the present moment, if only for the sake of being appreciative of and grateful for our influences. It's a central Buddhist practice to contemplate the preciousness of our life, which is essentially an exercise in acknowledging the beauty of the interdependence of the self. Whatever opportunities we've had (or missed) in life are due to a wide variety of factors, which can't be compartmentalized and segregated. Whatever creative inspiration we have in life comes from a multitude of sources.

Hopefully we have all had at least one teacher of some kind whom we respect, maybe revere, and are grateful for. Where would we be—no, *who* would we be—without even one of our good teachers? Or one of our bad teachers, for that matter? What if even one of our life's traumas hadn't happened? The very structure of our identity would look different; our river of self would be flowing in an unfamiliar direction. If I'm constantly lamenting my past, wishing that an embarrassing event never happened, or wishing I'd never made the mistake of falling in love with a certain person, in effect what I'm wishing is that I *had never happened*. This type of remorse always denies the interdependence of one's own identity—which brings us back to inadequacy.

Real insight, useful insight, comes from deepening our understanding of the interdependence of the self. That kind of understanding begins to counteract both inadequacy and arrogance. Contemplating the complexity of our own identity helps to develop appreciation for where we came from, the people and environments that helped us flourish and the obstacles we faced. It's possible that even those dark and scary parts of our mind could be incorporated into the tapestry and utilized if we fully recognize ourselves as interdependent beings.

At the same time, humility develops from viewing ourselves as interdependent, liquid selves. If we look closely, we can't really take full credit for the things we've accomplished in life. As a river receives its water from other sources, we each plagiarize and borrow from the past. Our accomplishments are the results of puzzle-pieces falling into the right place at the right time. We are standing on the shoulders of our ancestors, our families, our mentors and friends.

While our intelligence is definitely *ours*, it comes through the cradled support of countless predecessors. We are always responding to the past, however independent of any human lineage we wish we were. Keeping this in view pops the useless balloon of arrogance, the need to be better than anyone else.

The other crucial point of contemplating interdependence of the self is seeing how much we suffer and how much suffering we cause by *not* noticing the complexity of our identity. We get smacked in the face constantly, thinking we are one prefabricated thing, like one of those Lego statues viewed from far away. And we continually lash out against others as a preemptive strike against the threat of our fixed identity being challenged.

Interestingly enough, one of the times that we see with great clarity how attached we are to narrow definitions of ourselves is when we're insulted or challenged. Experiences arise that are outside the comfort zone of who we are willing to allow ourselves to be. When we pay attention, this happens so often it's comical. You hope you're a great artist, until another gallery rejects your work. You pride yourself on your basketball skills, until someone half your age schools you on the court. You consider yourself a very mindful person, then someone catches you daydreaming.

Whenever we fixate on maintaining a solid static identity, image becomes *everything*. A teenager begging entry into the cool kids' clique can't tell anyone he loves role-playing games. A punk might have a hard time relaxing among the crowd at a hip-hop show. A progressive who suddenly realizes that those kind and considerate people he's been eating dinner with are in fact Republicans will probably feel a bit uneasy. This solid tendency to identify ourselves strikes us even if we think we're not into promoting our own image. Then we can't stand to be surrounded by people who care so much about their goddamn image!

A river doesn't have this problem. It doesn't get pissed off if the unknown waters of new experience enter its mouth. The Hudson doesn't waste its time wishing it were a classier river, like the Seine or the Nile. It doesn't get angry at the Ganges for having different landscapes along its banks. But we compare our identities constantly, trying to triangulate ourselves with the right interests, preferences, and associations. The real problem is this: the more tightly we grip our constructed identities, the less flexible we are in the face of change and challenge, and so the spectrum of experience that we just can't accommodate broadens. Our comfort zone constricts, and we become less and less willing to experience anything that occurs even an inch outside what is familiar and acceptable. In the quest for independence of the self, we try to fit ourselves into such a tight box of identity that it becomes a prison, a depressing coffin of frozen self-image.

The problem with the myth of our personal independence—as well as the myth of our permanence—is that it takes a ton of time and energy to continuously fortify the dam of our identity, to make it strong enough to withstand the overwhelming pressure of truth's fluid nature. Thankfully, reality's job is to expose the places where our self-image has frozen over. No makeshift dam we can build will last long; the forceful waters of new experience always burst through. But in most moments when our fixed identity is called into question, we miss the message. Instead of seeing that we are much more than the simplistic creations we thought, we just try to rebuild the dam of rigid identity on the basis of familiar habit. We get defensive or we get angry at the critics who called our identity into question. The ego—the state of mind that gets caught up in the myth of solid independence—pollutes the hell out of the river.

LOOKING AT OUR OWN IDENTITIES and starting to encounter the myth of our personal independence, it's also dangerous to go too far in the confusing direction of "no-self." When we get into this territory of nonexistence, things quickly get murky. A lot of New-Age philosophies take something that looks like the truth of interdependence and proclaim the vaguest statement of all: "We are all ONE." It is as if our collective consciousness were some amorphous cosmic borscht, and the point of spiritual practice is to melt back into the luminous goo from which we all came, sighing in a vague and final ecstasy. But that's not what interdependence of the self is pointing toward at all.

Who we are is of course dependent on and interwoven with the identities of those who share our life and our world.

While acknowledgement of interdependence of the self requires coming to terms with our false fixation on a constructed identity, it doesn't mean that we don't exist as individuals. We are each living, breathing, and loving in our own assorted ways, with our matchless snowflake-patterns of idiosyncrasies. In fact, interdependence of the self is what guarantees that each of us is a *completely unique* individual. We are all connected and dependent on each other, but we are not in any way the *same* individuals. No two of us have had exactly the same multitude of events carrying us into the here and now. In this present moment there is only one me and only one you.

When we discuss the interdepen~~~
one way to explore the idea of egoless~
apparent contradiction. Egolessness ~~
Rather, egolessness can be fully equated with the ~~
pendence of the self. Egolessness is therefore what *makes us exactly who we are.* Like the connection between the Hudson and the Seine, we aren't all just the same amorphous bodies of water, but we also aren't nearly as separate as we tend to believe.

Regardless of any philosophy, we all know that we will have to wake up tomorrow and face the other people in our life, interact with our community, and take part in the world. At that point, the outer levels of interdependence begin to manifest. But if we have a method for staying in touch with the multifaceted, prismatic, and fluid nature of our own identity, we'll be much better equipped to deal with other people.

INTERDEPENDENCE IN RELATIONSHIPS

When we begin to explore ourselves in connection to and in dependence upon the people we know personally, we are examining the next level outward: interdependence in relationships.

Understanding interdependence in relationships extends straight from the logic of the interdependence of the self. Viewing ourselves as interdependent will necessarily grant us a greater ability to witness the interdependence of *other* selves. Because it's not just this thing called ME that is an interdependent self. The people around you must be governed by

.ne exact same principle. Each being we know is a shifting accumulation of events, impulses, emotions, perspectives and values. Seeing this is especially helpful whenever difficulties come up in our personal relationships.

We often mistakenly view the people in our life as solid entities, as if we were playing with them like the pieces on a chess board. Our family is the king; our lover the queen; our bosses or teachers, the bishops; our friends, the rooks; our coworkers or creative partners are the knights, and all of the extras in our daily routine are the pawns. We try to move each person, each piece, in certain set patterns. They each offer us certain types of security and unique kinds of headaches, playing particular roles in the ongoing chess match of life. Viewed this way, relationships tend toward predictable patterns of interaction, moving in long-established arcs of communication and conflict. In chess, a pawn can only make certain moves, and a knight can only jump two ahead and one to the side, again and again, predictably.

Similarly, we get caught thinking we know the people in our life for good, how we're going to be around them, what we're going to say to them, how they are going to respond to us. We think they'll know how we're going to be around them, we'll know what they're going to think, we'll know exactly who they're going to be.

A few months ago I decided to have a heart-to-heart talk with a close friend. It was one of those moments in life where I thought I saw something very clearly about someone I cared for. I decided to give her—out of love and respect—an in-depth description of who she is. I mean, who she really is. Rambling through my perceptions of her, I told her she was too humble, too serious, and too logically minded. In the middle of my diatribe, she burst out laughing. Earlier in the day, she had also gotten a supportive earful from another close friend (her stars must've been in the right alignment for lectures). Except, in the words of her other friend, her problems were that she was a bit bold and arrogant, too much of a comedian, and never detail-oriented enough.

Maybe one of her two friends was crazy, or just plain wrong. More likely, some of what we each had to say about our mutual friend contained some truth. This is because who we are in each of our relationships isn't just about us—it's about the mingling of our personality with the other person's.

We are different around our fathers than around our mothers, different with old high school friends than people we work with. We don't address a police officer quite the way we address a priest. Why? Because the truth of who we *are* invariably depends upon who we are *with* at the present moment, and vice versa. Each relationship has its own life, its own clumsy dance, its own dialect and subtle body language. This truth may be obvious, but we often ignore the implications of it.

We often fall into the trap of talking about our relationships as if people do things *to* or *for* each other. Usually we get absorbed with thinking about what other people are doing to or for *us*. But a relationship is not what happens *to* people or *for* people. Relationships happen *between* people, interdependently. When we scrutinize our relationships, it's hard to say exactly who is doing what to/for whom. This is because the participants in any relationship are co-producing the bond between them, and are mutually responsible for each step in their dance.

I know from my own experience that, in an argument, there's a mental tendency to place the blame squarely on the shoulders of just one of the participants. If I'm wracked with guilt, I might take all the blame. Otherwise it's all the other person's fault.

So I call a third person to tell her the story from my point of view, seeking outside confirmation that the person I'm fighting with is in fact, objectively speaking, a true and complete asshole. I might think the third person is a "good" friend if she confirms my righteousness—but really, an even better friend would probably question my static point of view.

The person I'm having my issue with might not be getting into the same kind of problem with other people he knows. On the other hand, maybe he is, and as we find out that other people have the same issues with him, it helps us see something clearly about someone we care about. Still, if we want to have positive relationships with others, we're going to need to relinquish our eternal claim on righteousness, and our illusion of isolated independence; we have to admit that any personal dispute is partially created by what we ourselves are bringing to the relationship. Interdependence implies that any relationship has no existence whatsoever outside of the joint custody of all of the people who create it and give it life. Problems come up between people, not independent of them. Relationships are tangled, sticky webs—messy zones of mutual responsibility.

The important point is deepening our understanding of how communication between people really works. This becomes especially important in dealing with anger. (More on anger in chapter 7.) Examining interdependence on a relational level brings greater awareness to all the subtle and not-so-subtle effects we have on the people in our life. Without this awareness, we can become unbelievably manipulative. Maybe those other people really are assholes (objectively speaking) but maybe they also have deeply complex, painful histories that they carry with them which inform their "asshole-ness." And truthfully, maybe so do we.

INTERDEPENDENCE AND COMMUNITIES

The Buddhist word for community is *sangha*. It usually refers to a group of people who come together to practice Buddhism. More generally, it means a group of people who gather for any common cause, who share a common space, or rely on each other for a certain service. From this point of view, within the larger world of our city or town, each of us is involved in many sanghas, a variety of communities that crisscross and intersect each other. Neighborhood, school, work, and extended family each constitute a sangha. The art world is a sangha; the yoga world is a sangha; the NBA is a sangha.

The main distinction between interdependence in relationships and in communities involves each individual's understanding of his role in the unfolding of communal activity. It's easier to contemplate the effects of our actions on the people to whom we personally relate—although sometimes we'd rather not think about it. Within communities, the effect an individual has on the larger community is much more hidden. Community is the first place where the ripple effects of an individual's presence might not be noticeable to that individual.

For this reason, it's very easy to ignore interdependence in communities. When we crave isolation, it becomes all too convenient to forget that we actually do exist in sanghas: I drop a candy wrapper on the street and don't think about who might pick it up, or where it might go if no one picks it up. I get on a bus and forget to say thank you to the bus driver, the human being who's helping me get to wherever I'm in such a hurry to be. You have a party and play music so loud it causes your neighbor's wall to pulsate. Or maybe you're hyper-sensitive to every little sound and call the police every time the neighbors have even a few people over for dinner, without reflecting whether this is necessary. We walk the streets with our heads down low, afraid to break anonymity with the other members of our neighborhood sangha, trapped in the assumption that they're crazy or dangerous, or somehow have nothing to do with us. Ignorance of interdependence on the community level is really an out-of-sight, out-of-mind kind of situation.

There are some small towns where everybody knows everybody. In Dar es Salaam, Tanzania, a friend of mine found that many local residents could not believe that New Yorkers remain completely unknown to their next-door neighbors in the same building! "How is that possible?" they kept asking her. Meanwhile, in a place like Los Angeles, community is what happens when two solitary drivers glare at each other through windshields on the freeway. When we aren't personally acquainted with the beings who make up our community, the truth of interdependence becomes an abstraction. And when the connections between us become abstract, we start to doubt they exist. And when that doubt settles in like a rolling fog, we shrug away our responsibility to others. The key is to expand awareness of the ripple effects that our actions have on the community at large. In my experience, meditation is easily the best way to prepare for this expansion of awareness.

INTERDEPENDENCE ON THE SOCIETAL LEVEL

When you were a little kid, did you have a hard time understanding the idea of countries? It's nearly impossible to remember how we conceived of planet Earth before words like America, Japan, France, and Ghana were drilled into our heads. I used to open my Mom's beat-up atlas and follow a map of the world several inches (and a few thousand miles) away from Manhattan. I'd trace the Southwestern U.S., come back to our tiny island of twenty-two square miles and go the same distance away in different directions—to Mexico, then Canada, then Europe and Africa.

With the kind of numerical logic available only to a child, I was convinced that I should probably care exactly the same amount about all of the people in each of those places, because they were the exact same number of inches and miles away from my finger. In my mind, there was direct relationship between the radius of distance and the radiance of love. But people on TV told me—in no uncertain terms—that I was supposed to care about people in the U.S. more than those in any other place. We were all Americans, and the folks in Mexico and Europe were not. They were They. They were not US. End of story. I didn't understand that at that all. Frankly, I still don't.

On the global level, the truth of interdependence is the most distant and abstract. It is also the most pressing. The main difficulty in recognizing interdependence globally is seeing the effects that actions we take as individuals will have on people we will probably never meet, never touch, never share intimate space with. Yet global interdependence tells us that the air which leaves our lungs in our next exhalation will eventually become the inhalation of someone five thousand miles away. The truth of interdependence may be hidden from sight moment by moment, but that doesn't mean it isn't real.

When we expand the vision of interdependence even further, we can see the way that the billions of people alive are "co-producers" of planet Earth. This thing we call "The World" is actually the interdependent product of all the fears, hopes, assumptions, biases, value judgments, creativity, and—most of all—*actions* of the billions of people who inhabit it. As individuals, our minds help to project the state of the world we live in. Like the butterfly effect in chaos theory, the truth of interdependence states that no individual's action merely disappears into outer space without any effect. Each action creates the grounds for some situation that follows it. If I notice that my actions always arise initially from my state of mind, then it becomes clear that the hate-filled thought that I just can't let go of might somehow affect somebody living thousands of miles (and just a few inches) away.

Discussions about the societal level of interdependence are already happening, mostly without any help from Buddhist philosophy. The issues that happen to be closest to my heart are the insanities of global wealth distribution, the obsolescence of war, and the crisis of global warming. This book would have to be ten thousand pages long to even initiate a specific discussion of most global or societal issues of interdependence. It would also have to be written by a more qualified person.

The purpose here is to invite an inner paradigm shift away from isolation—to draw attention to the very real link between each of our minds and the way this world we share operates and manifests. It is vital—crucial—that we remember such a link is ever-present, even if we can't always see it in our everyday life. Interdependence requires us to develop an individual consciousness that views our society through a lens transcending boundaries of states and countries. We must also develop a worldview that consistently takes responsibility upon ourselves. The problems of the world—wherever they occur—never belong to Someone Else. The buck stops here.

UNIVERSAL INTERDEPENDENCE

Interdependence is not only about the physical world. It's also about the world of concepts and ideas. Like people or events, no idea that can be expressed through language exists outside of a web of connections. Interdependence is truly universal. It describes all relationships: all this-or-thats, all dualistic oppositions, all concepts and ideas that stand in relationship to each other. In other words, there is no label which resides independently of the other labels to which it stands in relationship. "Rich" and "Poor" never stand alone.

They are conceptual denominations that rely on each other for their relative existence. Until you label someone "rich," you have nothing to contrast the experience of "poor" against. For example, a millionaire could claim the psychological status of a "poor" person whenever he looks up at billionaires (and some do). Likewise, someone who by today's standards would be lower-middle class in Europe would be living the lifestyle of luxury equivalent to that of an opulent duke in the middle ages. Rich implies a side-by-side comparison to that which is simultaneously poor. One label creates the definition of its opposite.

As soon as you say that something is good or virtuous, you are simultaneously creating the idea of evil. The two cannot be separated without losing their relational meaning completely. This is why wars happen. No matter how hard we try to construct a rigid moral code of right and wrong, good and evil, us and them, we're just trying to place labels on an unbounded, liquid reality. It's like trying to put a sticky note on a river so that we will always remember what the river is—as well as what it is *not*, what is *other* than the river. Meanwhile, the ink on the sticky note quickly dissolves and the note just floats away downstream.

Universal interdependence is a synonym for another Buddhist concept: *emptiness.* There is nothing, on any level—physical or conceptual—that exists independently of that which stands in relation to it. All concepts are empty of independent existence. But this emptiness certainly does not mean that concepts aren't real entities with real implications in the physical world. In fact, the whole idea of meditation is to demonstrate that the hidden structures of our concepts have a much stronger impact on our life than we ever realized.

Another way that Buddhist philosophy discusses emptiness is by pointing out the relationship between an external
event and the minds that perceive (and create!) that event.
For instance, if the BBC and Fox News both cover the same
story, they will probably each deliver a radically different
perspective on what happened. This is because it's impossible to separate what actually occurs from the biased
minds that witness it. Thus, the mind and the phenomena
the mind perceives are each "empty" of, or without, their
own singular existence. The perceiver and the events perceived are forever in union, universally interdependent.

Emptiness might seem like a strange word-choice: after
all, the universal level of interdependence could just as easily be thought of as *fullness* or *completeness*. Everything that
happens or might happen is accommodated in the real
Internet of interdependence. Thus, interdependence con-
stitutes a very "full" description of reality. There's a surpris-
ing interplay between emptiness and completeness. A
universal lack of independent existence is coupled with the
fullness of possibility that anything and everything can
happen, should the right causes and conditions develop.
There is a constant back-and-forth between the fact that
nothing exists independently and the fact that all possibilities can come into being within this brilliant Internet.
These two concepts are deeply wedded—and they have a
hyphenated name: Emptiness-Luminosity.

THESE FIVE LEVELS OF INTERDEPENDENCE:
the self, relationships, community, society, and universal
interdependence, are useful categories for contemplation.
But the million-dollar question is this: How can we begin
to move through life with an increased awareness of how

our actions impact, and are impacted by, all of these levels simultaneously?

Those of us who would *really* like to see the world become truly kinder and gentler often fall into the trap of narrowly focusing on only one of the levels of interdependence at the expense of the others. Karl Marx has always been a startling example of this trap for me. A man who had grand global visions of a society no longer based on greed or aggression was—by many subjective accounts—a negligent father and husband. If we long to save the whole world but we can't deal with our own family and friends, something has gone wrong in our understanding of what it means to be human.

When the ancient Indian Buddhist master Padmasambhava was asked what it felt like to be enlightened, he said: "My mind is as vast as the sky. My actions are as fine as a grain of sand."

Padmasambhava was describing interdependence, and how he could move through life recognizing it, stretching his awareness both inward and outward at the same time. His mind had simultaneously become both more vast and more precise, larger and smaller. He was seeing more of the refined details and having greater vision of the construction of the larger system. He was thinking globally, acting locally.

In fact, interdependence is the ultimate "think globally, act locally" perspective. It begins with us and radiates outward. If it doesn't begin with us, then it becomes bobblehead chatter and thought-bubble theory. Huge steps are missing, with nothing to connect the dots between the minutiae of our momentary actions and the global scale of events. Talk and theory are fine—but only if action comes from them.

At the same time, our insight into interdependence must lead us somewhere that Buddhist philosophy has rarely gone in its history: we must deeply examine, critique, and transform the complexes of confusion and suffering that exist not only on the personal level, but on the systemic and societal level. If Buddhism has any relevance here and now, it must quickly develop both social and political applications.

THE OVERWHELMING NATURE and already-everywhere-ness of interdependence could make us feel unable to affect anything in a positive way. Sometimes it's hard just to make it through a day without breaking something or yelling at somebody, so it might be a lot to ask to begin viewing our world as a completely connected Internet of people, events, beings, and systems. Seeing interdependence can even lead us into depression. If we examined the ripple effects of every little thing we did, we'd see there is no way to be alive without causing at least some harm to ourselves and others. It might make us want to curl up into fetal position in a dark corner, afraid even to breathe due to the harm it would cause to microscopic organisms. We could come to believe that whatever we do is meaningless—or just plain harmful. So rather than paying attention to every word that flies out of our mouths, instead of concerning ourselves with how every tiny consumption choice we make could affect the Middle East or Africa, why not just grab a(nother) beer? Overwhelmed by the magnitude of this truth, we could forever acquiesce to habit and circumstance, waiting around for someone braver to make the first move of what seems an impossible journey.

Such nihilism comes from the subtle propaganda of thinking we're powerless. As Al Gore put it so clearly in *An*

Inconvenient Truth, witnessing interdependence should not lead us straight from denial into despair. There is a middle way: doing something.

Because it's impossible to cause zero harm in the world, we can relax and relinquish that quest for perfection—but this is in no way the same thing as giving up and getting shitfaced. One of the greatest lessons that comes from meditation is that a relaxed curiosity about life and sleepwalking through it are two radically different choices. Relaxation is perfect for the development of awareness of the effects of any of our actions and states of mind. We can definitely alter *some* of them in order to lessen the suffering we cause. We don't have to become hyper-conscious, über-neurotic champions of global interdependence—screaming righteously at everyone who drives SUVs, or feeling unbearably guilty about the horrific conditions under which our underwear was stitched. We can instead examine our actions and the system we live in with an inquisitive mindset.

Keeping a sense of humor about our own confusion, we can begin to link up with a larger human web of friends, communities, and societies. If we don't consistently choose to make these connections, we ignore the truth of our own life, and deny the manifest reality of our own world.

Mastering an understanding of interdependence means mastering a fluid domain of interwoven truth. There just isn't a static rulebook—as much as we might wish for one to tell us exactly *what* to do. Understanding interdependence means being aware of the shifting relativity of your own morality, without the blinding paralysis of righteousness.

Historically, Buddhism doesn't offer much advice on what to do to be mindful and compassionate in *specific* situations—and people sometimes find that lack of specific instructions frustrating. People ask questions like "What does Buddhism say about abortion?" Well, I could lend my personal interpretation of abortion given my own ongoing contemplation of Buddhist principles, but you'd still have to make a decision for yourself.

Buddhism is a tradition of general principles for how to train one's mind and how to hold that mind in the realm of daily action. These instructions are conveyed primarily through analogy, stories, and many categorized mappings of different qualities of the mind. If we want concrete advice for specific instances in our actual life, we can often be frustrated by Buddhism's answers (or lack thereof). But anyone who claims to have a manual for living our present life in this society is in possession of an out-of-date edition. Nobody has ever lived this life before. And this moment is brand new, so there couldn't be any Lonely Planet guide to navigating it.

If what you want is a rulebook for living your life, you're going to have to write it yourself—and then even your own hard and fast bullet-points will fade into impermanence, like that sticky note left to float on down the river.

THE FOLLOWING CHAPTERS use a classical Buddhist teaching called the Six Transcendent Actions (*Paramitas*)—meditation, generosity, discipline, nonviolence, exertion, and wisdom. Practicing these can increase our experience of interdependence on all of the five levels at once. And when that happens, the course of necessary action becomes selflessly evident.

PART TWO:
PRACTICING INTERDEPENDENCE

The trouble is that once you see it, you can't unsee it. And once you've seen it, keeping quiet, saying nothing, becomes as political an act as speaking out.   There's no innocence.   Either way, you're accountable.

ARUNDHATI ROY

Make sure when you say you're in it but not of it, you're not helping to turn this into the place sometimes called hell.

STEVIE WONDER

CHAPTER 4:
MEDITATION AND THE COLONIZING MENTALITY

Between thought and expression
lies a lifetime.

THE VELVET UNDERGROUND

THE WORD "PRACTICE" IS PROFOUND.
When we think of developing awareness of interdependence, it's crucial to view this as a practice. But in this
context, "practice" doesn't "make perfect." It implies a
process, not an outcome; an exploration, not an expectation. It would be a very different thing for a painter to wake
up in the morning and say "I'm going to practice painting
today, just grab the brushes and get to work," instead of
saying "If I don't have a solo gallery show in five years I'm
definitely going to slit my wrists." The first is a moment-
by-moment exploration, while the second is a harsh and
vague expectation.

A lot of us seem to have unbending five-year plans in
our minds. It's as if we've magically been given a look at our
future resumés, and now we need to follow the steps to

make it happen. When I find myself falling into this trap, I try to ask myself: *Did I have a five-year plan five years ago? Did everything go according to that plan? (Did anything?) Does it matter to me any more if my old five-year plan went comically awry? Do I even want to be the person dictated by the old plan any more? So why the hell am I making a new five-year plan in my head* right now?

The practice of interdependence is not about predicting the time and place of our final contentment, scheduling the precise details of our impending enlightenment. It's definitely not about envisioning the set design of the stage on which we will accept the award for singlehandedly saving the world. In the process of developing your understanding of anything, you will constantly encounter a friction between your hopeful expectations and the messy procession of what is actually unfolding in the present moment. To practice anything—whether it's meditation, art, or politics—means to keeping relinquishing the plan and to continually return to what's unfolding now.

On the Buddhist path, meditation is the central practice and the main support of this endeavor.

It can often look like meditation is about asserting and practicing our independence, not interdependence. From the outside, it might appear to be a self-involved, hermetically sealed, isolationist pursuit. Maybe we're escaping the world for the sake of developing peace of mind, entering our personal sensory-deprivation tank. It doesn't help this perception that an intensive period of meditation is commonly called a *retreat*, which is something armies do to try to escape a battle they know they can't win.

The history of Buddhism tells countless stories of practitioners who renounced mainstream society, either becoming monks and nuns, or going off to live in the rough solitude of deep forests or caves on the sides of unreachable mountains. In Tibetan Buddhism in particular, you'll repeatedly find the heroic stories of yogis who fled their homes and families, glad to have left the world behind.

In these stories, the monk or yogi usually proclaims his intentions for leaving his life behind with what seems a touch of arrogance: he simply has no more use for "worldly concerns." He will devote much or all of his life to solitary meditation. These stories somehow parallel the ideal of the American cowboy, applauding the John Waynes or Clint Eastwoods of Buddhism, the rugged individualists who set out to realize their own independence from everything—the ultimate self-sufficiency of mind. And in these narratives, this utter self-sufficiency would then become equated with enlightenment and full spiritual attainment.

On the surface, this doesn't sound much like a person trying to deepen her understanding of interdependence. Fewer and farther between are the tales of those who stayed in their mainstream lives practicing meditation, dealing directly with the truth of interdependence in their relationships, communities, and larger societies. But there are ancient examples of farmers, kings, queens, artisans, and laborers alike who all become master meditators without fleeing into lifelong retreat. Rarest of all in Buddhist history are the stories of social revolutionaries who used meditation as the cornerstone of their revolutionary—or evolutionary—paths. These heroes not only remained engaged in their societies, but also challenged the oppressive and confused social structures of their society. Thankfully, modern history has given us several powerful examples of Buddhist revolutionaries like Aung San Suu Kyi, Thich Nhat Hanh, and the Fourteenth Dalai Lama.

The Buddhist tradition talks a lot about helping people, and these teachings are studied by cave-dwelling yogis and social revolutionaries alike. There are many techniques of meditation explicitly designed to instill in the practitioner greater awareness and care for others. There is incredible power in the instructions for dissolving the dichotomy between self and other, so we can extend compassion beyond absorption with our own problems and needs. My friends, especially those who are interested in helping the world, say things like "So, remind me: how does sitting on your ass help anybody, exactly?" From the outside, meditation can seem mystical, indulgent, and weird.

It's a shame that Buddhism has permitted meditation to be consistently misbranded this way in our cultural consciousness. Meditation is often misperceived as an activity for the spiritual fringe of society or as a remedy of last resort, utilized only by people going through a crisis for whom nothing else has worked.

This view of meditation as a retreat from life is not helpful at all. The reason for meditating is to systematically and progressively bring the practitioner to a place where she or he is more and more able to live in the world.

It would, however, be naïve to say that meditation is not somehow self-involved. Of course it's self-involved. No matter how you spin it, the meditator is spending a period of time alone with his or her mind. But consider how we usually become self-absorbed in our daily routines—the litany of useless things we do with absolutely no purpose at all, like checking email every five minutes, surfing the Internet for hours searching for nothing in particular, or leafing absently through a magazine we've already read from cover to cover. Now *that's* being self-centered. Doing something intelligently self-involved is a lot more beneficial than the typical mindless activity. Doing something settling, clarifying, and introspective beats the hell out of watching another generic Hollywood movie (yet) again.

Of course, there's the other extreme to meditation, which is to set the bar of our intention outlandishly high. When people say their reason for meditating is to "free all sentient beings from suffering," it sounds a little grandiose, to say the least. Sometimes we chant this type of aspiration in a dead cultish monotone, and this really suspect, glazed aura hovers in our eyes. At best it looks like a group of folks regurgitating the text of a passé Buddhist Hallmark card, and at worst it looks like we're all about to drink the Kool-Aid.

Like anything else we do, practicing meditation becomes much more relevant if we remain in touch with a realistic motivation for doing it. Without it, any and every practice becomes clichéd, a rote operation, a spiritual monkey chained to a typewriter. And when difficulties arise in any practice, a plethora of justifications will bloom to explain why we can't find the time. Then the practice slips away, fading out into the ether of our murky inspiration, along with the remnants of a thousand other failed New Year's resolutions.

In meditation, frustrations and difficulties always arise eventually; this is true for everyone who practices. Frustrations are inevitable. So there is a deep need to stay in touch with the reasons meditation plays an important role in your life, how it helps you recognize interdependence. Otherwise, the practice will quickly become uninspired and futile.

Ultimately, meditation is a catalyst—it brings about a "chemical reaction" of change in the various elements that make up our life. When we meditate, we're putting ourselves directly in touch with the basic interface we have for experiencing our life and the world around us. We only have one wireless connection with the real Internet, and that's our mind. There isn't a single moment in our lives when our mind is not functioning as the basis of all our interactions—not even one. So it makes sense to train ourselves in the skilful operation of this basic interface. This is what meditation is for.

Meditation can show us the interdependence of the self, counteract the Inadequacy Principle, and ease those hollow voices of self-criticism. It might simply offer a little bit more calmness and clarity. But as the practice proceeds, we might begin to empathize more deeply with the people we stand in personal relationship to, and find some ways to bring the benefits of practice into our interactions with them. Maybe we'll start thinking about our community differently, and how our actions have tangible effects on society at large. You might even have a glimpse of your connection with all beings. And when that glimpse comes, why not raise the bar higher for your reasons for practice, and aspire to help everyone you encounter? Just stay grounded in the realities of your own life and your day-to-day interactions. The question of intention—of *why* we're meditating—is everything. Intention grows from deepening our understanding of how the products of our minds—our actions—ripple outward.

Contemplating interdependence has certainly made the practice of meditation much more relevant in my own life. Learning to deal with my mind has made me far more curious about the people around me. The world is a place more vibrant and creative almost every time I stand up from the practice. While it can be overwhelming to consider the effects of my actions, it is also incredibly empowering. This kind of inspiration can help you want to get out of bed in the morning. Part of the power of meditation is seeing that meaningful development doesn't require a sea change; usually it's just a one-degree shift in habitual direction. And this realization can be an antidote to feeling scattered, defeated, and totally disempowered. In bearing witness to our own potential, the reasons for working with our own mind become razor-sharp and urgent. This is the only way meditation becomes an ongoing part of life.

WHAT ARE WE ACTUALLY DOING when we meditate? How does practicing connect with the experience of interdependence? What skills does meditation develop?

To be clear, meditation is a practice best learned and developed in person with living teachers. Books and audio instructions can of course give helpful support, but you can't learn and maintain a meditation practice just from books. See the first appendix for some very basic instructions to get started, or pick up the book *Turning the Mind into an Ally* by Sakyong Mipham. While many meditation techniques are fairly simple, the subtleties of experiences that arise in the practice are too difficult to grasp without help from teachers. Too many people rely solely on media instead of human teachers and communities to develop their practice. So, with regard to meditation: Do try this at home, but please, please, *please* don't try it *only* at home.

THE THREE BASIC MENTAL FACULTIES that meditation practice works with are *mindfulness*, *awareness*, and *insight*.

Think of a video camera. In a lot of ways, our mind records our perceptions, our emotions, our thoughts, our philosophies, and our worldview like a video camera does. Our mind is our most basic tool for capturing the narrative of our life and the larger context in which we exist. We are each the subjective documentarians of our own existence.

MINDFULNESS

Mindfulness is what allows us to remain present with an experience long enough to familiarize ourselves with it. Mindfulness becomes relevant when we get that sinking suspicion that our personal camera is a little blurry and our mental cinematographer has a shaky hand. The camera swivels around with no rhyme or reason; we hear voices in the background but can't tell who's talking; then we space out and the camera frames a patch of the rug on the floor for long minutes at a time.

We need mindfulness to steady and focus, even a little bit. We usually mindlessly jump from object to object, from perception to perception, from idea to idea. Sometimes—within our cultural and personal Attention Deficit Disorder—we jump cut to seventeen different objects of perception in approximately five seconds, or we try to juggle seventeen different tasks at once. Because we're constantly leapfrogging around, we never have the chance to get familiar with the functioning of our mind. We don't notice how we perceive our thoughts or how unexamined assumptions are present within our perceptions.

An unstable mind with no connection to mindfulness and no ability to stay in one place is going to miss a ton of reality. It will cascade away from the present moment. An unstable mind returns to direct perceptions just enough to gather the basic information necessary to stay alive and keep the screenplay inside our head moving forward (somewhat) smoothly. Sometimes we only have direct mindful experience when our survival instinct kicks in. If you step into the street and almost get hit by a bus, then—thanks to adrenaline—you'll become deeply mindful of where you are and what you're doing.

Without mindfulness you can't have a clear picture based on direct experience. Mindfulness is crucial for a direct experience of *anything*—an experience that isn't just based on our ideas of things. And direct experience, in turn, is essential for seeing interdependence. Obviously, in a book, it's necessary to talk about interdependence theoretically, metaphorically, and through stories. The reality of interdependence, however, is not just about theorizing. It's about experiencing it as it happens, moment by moment. Mindfulness is the muscle that helps us do that. For most of us, our connection with direct experience is tenuous at best; there's no shame in admitting that. And all kinds of problems arise when we only have an on-and-off love affair with reality.

What actually happens in those moments when we're completely lost in our heads? What happens to a mind that isn't settled or curious enough to investigate things directly and stay put long enough to actually understand what is in the frame of experience? To keep the plot clear and consistent, we plug filler material into those missing moments where we've been MIA. To create this filler material, we have to make a lot of assumptions about what is happening, both within ourselves and in the world we inhabit.

The deadliest thing about most assumptions is that they reside outside our immediate consciousness. They become like whispered mantras. They form an invisible superstructure for the development of all of our thoughts and actions. They become the source code from which all of our beliefs are compiled. It's like looking at everything through a deep-blue lens: eventually you might get so used to it that you think that all color has a bluish tint. And that is precisely the root of ignorance.

When we start to assure ourselves that our assumptions definitely depict the truth, they become fortified into bullet-pointed ideology and bullet-proof dogma. The mind becomes enslaved, chained by a series of vague connections, images, and memories—evoked by the buzzwords of random thought. All we end up experiencing is the indirect idea of things—a hazy picture with low production values. And because the connection between an unexamined mind and direct experience is so flimsy, the power of persuasion over that mind is enormous. That mind can be easily sold lies—even by itself—and can mistakenly interpret those lies as universal truths. That's the colonizing mentality.

It may seem like a leap to link unquestioned assumptions to the colonizing mentality. It may seem too dismissive of the scope of human suffering, as we live in a world scarred by colonial oppression for many centuries. But we have to ask ourselves how the colonizers' work got started in the first place.

Simple moments of self-loathing and centuries of genocide do not operate on different principles. What distinguishes them are degree, scale, and scope. Each individual's tendency to live in the realm of assumptions slowly gets reified and collectivized. Eventually, the given aggressive assumption becomes a cultural *modus vivendi*.

As a self-identifying progressive person with family roots in the American South, I often can't fathom that my ancestors were connected to slavery, maybe were even slave-owners themselves. Yet I share the blood of these ancestors, so I must also share some of their genetic tendencies.

I always wondered what was going through the heads of the first Spanish conquerors who arrived on the coast of Africa in the sixteenth century. What could they have been thinking as they stormed into those villages and carted innocent people away into bondage? Often, history books don't spend much time examining the minds of the individuals who perform the atrocities. (It would be great if every history textbook had a chapter titled "What the Hell Were They Thinking?") To say they were just evil sons of bitches is too simplistic. To say they were shrouded under the belief that Africans were somehow *not even* people is much more informative.

Meditation lets us develop awareness of similar dogmatic tendencies—in much more innocuous forms—arising in our own minds. This awareness makes it increasingly impossible to categorize even the worst offenders with nondescript blanket statements like "evil."

The slavetraders didn't see suffering; they didn't even see *other human beings*. Through the filters of their unexamined dogma and self-importance, all they saw were doubloons and gold. That's what it means to live wrapped up in a concept, with no realization that we are dwelling in such a state. In a world pockmarked by oppression, greed, and hate, the first things to be colonized are the minds of individuals. Only later is the external world terrorized.

Mindfulness is the main method we have to counteract this human tendency. Dogma starts when we divorce ourselves from direct experience. Mindfulness is what returns us to it. Learning mindfulness necessarily involves learning to slow your mind down, learning to rest the attention on an object for long enough to become familiar with it. When you do this, you can remain with an experience long enough to understand it, to directly intuit its context or meaning, to not be enslaved by concepts that don't describe reality.

In its simplest form, mindfulness involves bringing the attention to engage with and rest upon specific objects. The reason for doing this is to consistently deepen our understanding of the contrast between (a) direct experience and (b) ideas, concepts, and beliefs that don't arise from direct experience. This does not mean that thoughts are bad. The point of meditation is not to empty the mind of thoughts—as if the mind were a trash can and thoughts were wadded-up tissues.

What is a thought, anyway? Why do we have them? Generally speaking, a thought is an attempt to articulate, categorize, and meaningfully communicate our direct experience. A thought is an attempt to bring context to our perceptions. There's nothing wrong with this. It actually seems incredibly intelligent and creative. After all, where would any of us be if we didn't have thoughts? I couldn't have written this book; every single sentence inked here emerged from the realm of thoughts. A few are more or less "mine" (interdependently speaking), and many thoughts were borrowed and reformulated from teachers and other influences.

So thoughts aren't the problem. Problems only develop

when thoughts no longer arise from or refer to actual experience. That's when thoughts start ossifying into their own bureaucratic institutions, becoming assumptions and dogma. And that's when the self-colonizing gets underway.

The basic training for witnessing the contrast between assumptions and direct experience starts with a chosen object for our attention. Often we use the breath. We could also pay direct attention to specific ideas or words (contemplative meditation), or mindfully extend our imagination to specific difficult circumstances (like *metta* or loving-kindness practices). We can also use specific images or symbols (visualization or mantra meditation). In any type of meditation, mindfulness is what steadies the frame of our mind. Of course, stillness and steadiness are relative terms. I have never practiced meditation without some movement in the mind—and fortunately for people like us, mindfulness isn't about being completely still or one-pointed. It is about settling down to find relative focus and clarity.

AWARENESS

When we start using mindfulness to hold ourselves in the frame of direct experience, we start noticing more of what is going on. *Awareness*—the second aspect of the mind developed by meditation—describes this ability to notice the larger context in which the present moment occurs. The basic idea of awareness is that as mindfulness steadies our camera hand, we *see* more of what is actually there, what filmmakers might call the *mise-en-scène* of the present moment.

Awareness can help us notice really simple contextual

elements. If you pay attention to the subway doors sliding open and all the people trying to get onto the car, you might become aware that you're standing in someone's way—and you might even step farther into the car. You might notice that you're actually angry at somebody (maybe even someone other than the person you're speaking angrily to), or that your friend just got a haircut. These are very simple examples of awareness at work. They all come from paying greater attention to the present moment, which is the work of mindfulness.

In formal meditation practice, we become intimately aware of the composition of our own thoughts, of the ideas rattling around in our heads. We can actually become aware of any thought we have, no matter how negative or difficult. This means that there is always something in our minds that is much bigger and more expansive than *any* specific thought, even in the midst of great anxiety or depression.

In truth, awareness never goes away; it is omnipresent. Awareness is bigger than confusion, because awareness is what *sees* confusion, recognizes it. Even simple moments of awareness are the best way to gain confidence that the human mind comes fully equipped with wisdom.

Through the willful repetition of a short, regular practice of mindfulness, awareness broadens and deepens. We start to notice set patterns of thoughts; we start to see the scaffolding of our assumptions. This can be a slow and sometimes painful process. You might start noticing very quickly how hard you always are on yourself, how nothing you do is ever good enough (especially your meditation practice). The Inadequacy Principle is the main filter we see through when we haven't trained in mindfulness.

INSIGHT

The third aspect of the mind trained in meditation is insight. This could be a really simple insight, like the ability to tell if it's appropriate to apologize to someone or time to look for a new place to live. It could be clearly seeing that you're being obnoxious. "I hate school" and "I need to break up with her" are actually moments of profound insight that I've had in meditation practice. Whatever the specific insight, it begins with the awareness born of clearly seeing the context of a mental pattern, and eventually leads into the slow process of stepping out of our engrained negative tendencies. Insights lead to those tiny shifts in action. Repeated moments of insight are what enable us to create those inner paradigm shifts that alter our approach to dealing with interdependence.

In traditional Buddhism, the main things we are said to gain insight into are "the nature of the mind" and "the nature of reality." These sound like grandiose concepts, but they're really deeper and more far-reaching applications of the same developed intelligence that can discern good hip-hop from bad spoken word, decent falafel from burnt chickpeas. As you develop insight into the nature of your mind, you attain a deeper understanding of the interdependence of the self. It's said that if we can actually stabilize and rest with this insight, our whole perspective changes, and we don't feel the need to defend our identity to the death. We also don't lose our mind when reality changes its plan.

It's said that the highest insight is clearly seeing the universal interdependence of all phenomena. This is when all the scaffolding of confusion, disconnection, and cynicism has finally collapsed. A Buddha lives full-time in this state, and all his or her actions therefore are rooted in a seamless direct experience of universal interdependence. This is the realization of emptiness-luminosity, the universal level of interdependence. This insight reveals the full connection of all events, ideas, and beings, as well as the fluid subjectivity of one's own identity within that network. Jorge Luis Borges describes this kind of insight in *The Aleph*: "I saw all the mirrors on Earth, and none reflected me." The mind is completely liberated from the bonds of confusion, free to act in the most beneficial and meaningful way available in any given circumstance: this is the deepest insight that comes from meditating.

In my own experience, regular meditation practice allows me to be more sane and present, so my life's not a swamp of depression, anxiety, and agitation. Because it works with the basic interface of the mind, the benefits of meditation come into play at every other point in each and every day.

THE REMAINING CHAPTERS address what are called post-meditation practices. Post-meditation is Buddhism's fancy name for the rest of your life—those twenty-three hours and forty-five minutes each day when you're not meditating. How we practice in these situations is crucial to a life lived in connection with the truth of interdependence. These practices and courses of action are based on the gradual development of mindfulness, awareness, and insight.

CHAPTER 5:
THE HUNGRY GHOST IS A SHADOW PUPPET

The only thing we own is our attachment.

SAKYONG MIPHAM RINPOCHE

AS OF EARLY 2007, there are over 700 billionaires in the world. This tiny group of people controls more wealth than the poorer half of humanity. That means there are 700 people who collectively control more material wealth than almost 3.5 billion other human beings. That's approximately 5 million poor people for each billionaire's wealth. It's a funhouse mirror, distorted to the millionth degree. It's hard to dream of any ethical basis for that inequality, hard to wrap one's mind around the functioning of a system of financial compensation for individual effort that allows and even congratulates this outcome.

For those of us somewhere in the middle (though most of the people reading this are much closer to the top of the ladder than we might realize), it's easy to ignore this truth because we are so caught up in our own meager struggles for ever-elusive comfort. Most of us are just trying to scrounge enough money to afford whatever lifestyle we want to lead right now. That alone takes too much time and energy to worry about all the billionaires and impoverished billions. Most of the time, I'm too busy trying to score a nicer apartment and a good Thai restaurant to worry about people in Uganda who make my monthly rent in a year. I can't even stretch my mind to worry about the poor people in my own neighborhood most of the time.

When we talk about interdependence, the issues of wealth and economics have to come up. If every single event happens in dependence upon other factors and conditions, how do I ever determine what is "mine," exactly? Within an understanding of change and fluidity, what does it even mean to hold something as my possession? How does an understanding of interdependence change the psychology of ownership? Whatever I claim as mine is clearly a result of what others have done, as well as what I have "earned." So how do I come to value and own things, and how do I cling to them? If the pair of shoes I wear right now are only placed on my feet by the toil of a group of overworked women in Asia, and laced up by the people who were generous enough to pay me for my labor, at what point do the shoes become mine instead of theirs?

Interdependence makes us examine how resources are created, utilized, and distributed in our relationships, communities, and of course, our global society. Obviously, so much of the manifestation of our world is a result of the psychological perception of value—how objects and services (and people) are imbued with relative worth. From a Buddhist perspective, the question of economics requires looking at how the mind itself reifies value. How do conscious beings come to infuse the objects of their experience with numerical judgments of relative weight and importance? What steps do we take to produce, possess, and keep whatever objects, services, or lifestyles our habitual perceptions deem as valuable?

THE AMERICAN MEDIA usually treats unfathomable accumulations of wealth as something to be applauded and envied. Billionaire status is something to dream about, private jets are something to try to hitch rides on, not something to critically examine. It would be interesting if the New York Times Real Estate section, for example, reported Rupert Murdoch's recent purchase of the most expensive apartment sold in NYC history ($44 million in 2005 for a triplex apartment) alongside a report of how much low-income housing could've been bought for that same sum of money. Of course, it didn't. Instead, the Times followed the usual "Lifestyles of the Rich and Famous" formula for reporting real estate deals, intended to make the readers wish they were Mr. Murdoch, instead of making the readers wish Mr. Murdoch knew just a little bit more about the practice of generosity.

You probably give at least some of your time, money, or energy to causes and organizations that you believe in. From this conventional standpoint, you are probably pretty generous already—and consistently volunteering your time or donating your money is indeed part of the traditional practice of generosity. Yet a deeper, more fundamental exploration of the practice of generosity has to do with understanding our consumption. First and foremost, generosity is not about what we give, but about how we take. Consumption and offering come together like a one-two punch. So, before we can really talk about *offering*, we have to look closely at the mentalities that fuel our *taking*.

Why do you buy what you buy, own what you own, live how you live? Which things in your life are really invaluable necessities, and which are disposable luxuries? What effects do your consumption choices have on people around you, and the world? These are important questions to challenge ourselves with on a daily basis.

Our individual and collective worldviews regarding generosity have been conditioned by certain assumptions. We operate under given beliefs about what we need for our own survival according to the manner to which we have—or would like to—become accustomed. These ideas directly affect how much we can offer to others.

Our consumption is conditioned on a deeper level by the very idea of "ownership" over the objects that make up our personal experience of life. And on the deepest level, the contemplation of our consumption leads us to explore our basic assumptions about what it really means to be happy and fulfilled.

THE DARK SIDE of consumerism is told in Buddhism's stories of "hungry ghosts." A hungry ghost is a kind of zombie who wanders in a massive desert, scouring the cracked sand for anything decent to eat. His eyes are vacuum cleaners, his stomach is the size of a blimp, and he salivates like one of Pavlov's dogs. Every once in a while he sees a lonely oasis with luscious fruit. Each time he finds an oasis, he thinks his luck has finally, permanently changed. This oasis is a good metaphor for our malls.

There's only one little problem—thanks to the inherited genes of his sad karmic state, the hungry ghost's throat is the width of a pencil. He could never consume enough to satisfy his gargantuan belly. Ever. But it doesn't stop him from trying, from shopping all over that ragged desert. He scours and scours, not because he needs to, but because it is what he's so *used* to doing. He assumes that there's nothing more to be than a consumer, nothing else to do with his time but shop. Through this engrained perception, he brings tremendous suffering to himself and others as he forages for each fleeting fix.

Overcoming consumerism—learning how to be receptive—doesn't mean owning *nothing* or getting rid of all of our stuff. Let's face it: stuff is nice. Material possessions can enrich our lives. Denouncing all objects would be a tremendously cynical and masochistic way to live. At one point in his journey to understanding interdependence, the historical Buddha is said to have tried this type of self-denial. It didn't work.

Denouncing all possessions seems like a logical first step on a journey to overcoming fixation. Once we start questioning our desire to consume and our incessant need for sensory gratification, the first reaction may be to denounce the *objects* of our experience *themselves*. Seeing the pain of our insatiable craving, we might want to quit consumerism cold turkey. Going too far in the other direction, we get deeply resentful of *stuff itself*. If I notice how much I am attached to my iPod and how much difficulty that attachment is causing (especially when it breaks or gets erased) my first response might be "better get rid of the iPod." The Buddha—as well as many other Asian Buddhist practitioners throughout history—tried giving away everything that might cause him to crave. It was a test of the very limits of his endurance. For a while, Shakyamuni practiced a level of self-mortification that might make Navy SEALs cringe.

During this period of stringent denial, he probably felt constant guilt every time he even felt hunger or thirst, howling inside at his own weakness of mind, his inability to conquer his senses. He must've felt he was failing miserably at his practice of overcoming the consumerism of six-century B.C.E. India. Finally, though, he had to give up this ascetic practice. His self-mortification wasn't leading to fulfillment; it brought no ease. It was too extreme, too cynical toward human nature. He realized that his sense perceptions and his quest for fulfillment were an integral part of being human. If he *really* weren't supposed to enjoy good food every once in a while, why had he been granted the priceless gifts of teeth and taste buds, smell and stomach? Was the spiritual path really about pretending he didn't have taste buds? Denying himself *any* enjoyment finally felt more like ignorance than wisdom.

The problem as such isn't the desire—for food, or an iPod, or even a pimped-out Beemer. In fact, schools of Buddhist thought hold that the root of the desire to consume is actually the intelligent ability to discern beauty and meaning within the objects of our experience. Desire is both natural and wise. It's normal to want to be in touch with beautiful, artful, and useful objects in order to experience their unique texture and brilliance. This includes our desire to be in touch with other people—a.k.a. attraction. It's only when we think there's a way to actually *possess* the external world of objects and perceptions—to forever reify our momentary experiences and earn some kind of cosmic interest on our investments—that we run into big fat problems. That's when we create problems for other people as well.

When that desire to connect with our senses is misunderstood, we become frenetic, fixated. The impulse to consume takes over and goes on a slow rampage through our minds. Over time this misunderstanding takes on perverse distortions. The mind begins to perceive the value of external objects based on fearful and increasingly warped habits, instead of the direct experience of their momentary beauty and purpose. How else could something like a dress worn at the Oscars come to be valued at a higher price than many people on Earth will see from all the labor they perform in their entire lifetime? How could the mechanism of this thing called the market allow a dress to have higher value than a human being's lifetime of toil? This perversion happens when the minds of the beings who create the market have become fixated on a distorted mode of perceiving value, altering human worth to tragic extremes. We've entered the desert of the hungry ghosts.

In this desert, suffering becomes intense and hard to stop, a self-perpetuating cycle. Consumerism is an addiction, incredibly deep and devastating. The devastation is this: what we're addicted to is not even one specific thing. We can't just conquer the addiction by removing ourselves cold turkey. Within the clutches of consumerism, what we're addicted to is cyclically feeling and assuaging that recurrent moment of WANT itself. It's not what we're shopping for that we get attached to, it's the need to shop, to acquire, itself. Consumerism is not one choice we make, one thing we buy. It is the result of an incessant inner terror that we drown out with a habit of WANTing, an unending spree at the Hungry Ghost Mall of America.

Of course, this moment of WANT has to attach to and express itself through specific choices and specific lifestyles.

Effective advertising moves the intuitive natural moment of directionless WANT in specific (profitable) directions depending on what kind of lifestyle we're pursuing. But the moment of WANT actually precedes the object it presently fixes upon. This is why desire is so easy to direct into strange and selfish consumption choices.

If you can give direction to an impulse that is inherently directionless, you can always become a highly successful salesman. The good news, on the other hand, is that the inherently directionless nature of the moment of WANT is the very reason it's possible to train our minds to become more receptive—to need less, to end our consumerism. If we practice becoming more deeply familiar with the moments of WANT, we'll gradually become lower-maintenance human beings.

The hungry ghost image contains a key for understanding the relative nature of wealth in the twenty-first century. What it means to be rich or poor is not at all measured against the basic standard of satisfying human needs. Instead, it's measured in terms of the Inadequacy Principle, always trying to find more because we are terrified of the daunting possibility of having less. This terror clutches us regardless of our personal rung on the socio-economic ladder. The mentality of poverty can and does strike at anyone and everyone, even though the physical reality of the kind of poverty that prevents the fulfillment of basic human needs only affects some (a very large "some"). That underlying fear of not having enough—our inner hungry ghost—haunts our thoughts, forever reminding us that we might not be able to reach or maintain our ideal lifestyle.

Everyone's just trying to keep up with our own Joneses, no matter who the Joneses are or what lifestyle they represent. Even billionaires are just trying to keep up with the Gateses and sheiks. Our inner hungry ghost tells us there *just isn't enough for us*, not enough oases in this whole endless desert called reality to make us feel sufficient. It tells us to rush to find that next lonely shopping spot and just get some MORE. Hurry while supplies last!

Take a look at where the hungry ghost lives: the desert. In terms of interdependence, the hungry ghost co-*creates* the desert. Again, the mind of an individual and the world inhabited by that individual always arise interdependently. The desert perpetuates the ghost's lonely state of vacuous consumption, which in turn perpetuates the desert—a most vicious cycle. We bleed the earth dry and wonder where all our lush resources went, then just as soon forget about what we've done and seek another fix. The sinister thing is that when we're feasting at one of the lonely oases, we don't have much meaningful awareness of the desert we've co-created around us.

My home city of NYC has always proved to be a profound example of the strange workings of this vicious mentality of poverty. In the 1980s, the streets of the city with the most wealthy people in the wealthiest country on Earth were also the reluctant home to over one hundred thousand homeless people. This was an absolutely mind-boggling fact—and for me as a child, the only way to deal with it on a daily basis was to pretend that either (a) it somehow wasn't actually happening or (b) it was somehow completely "natural" for an American city to be that way. Even those of us lucky enough to be karmically situated in an oasis usually can't enjoy what we have, and we tragically help spread the desert farther and wider.

THE NEED TO MAXIMIZE personal profit at all costs is what creates the desert of the hungry ghost. The profit mentality says: "Each time this wheel of fortune goes around, let me extract from the collective resources of society slightly more than whatever I put in. Let me always make a little more than I offer. Maybe even a lot more. This is, after all, the real way for all of us to be happy."

From the point of view of interdependence, we could see how this frame of mind—which neoclassical economics claims is the truly "natural" state of the human psyche—would consistently strip the shared resources of the individuals who inhabit such a community. The hungry ghost has been trying to maximize his own profit for so long that he turned what was once a garden into a desert. And then he forgot he did it! To paraphrase Sakyong Mipham Rinpoche, if happiness were about having the most stuff, then those of us who live in the world's wealthiest countries should be deeply, truly, unbelievably happy by now. Are we?

Questioning our consumption on a daily basis isn't just a good idea—it's a necessity. Finding the reasonable limits of human intake is Global Dilemma #1 for twenty-first century Earth. Oil, water, and fertile soil: you name it and we're losing it—and fast. If those of us in wealthier countries don't wean ourselves off the drug of consumerism, the earth is going to turn into a wasteland quickly. Meanwhile, we'll be too busy fighting over the shrinking oases to care what's happening to anyone else.

Buddhism's contribution to the crisis of consumerism doesn't begin with examining policies or advertising or theories of transnational corporations, although it definitely has something to say to those larger issues. It begins where our minds begin—on the level of the interdependence of the self—with us examining our personal consumption from the point of view of mindfulness and awareness. To actually alter our impact, we as individuals need to learn how these personal moments of WANT function at the mental source, and how to deal with them more sanely. Responsible consumption might very well be the key to saving planet Earth.

BUDDHIST PRACTICE offers no vaccination for the arising of WANT. Personally, I WANT a new iPod every time a new model comes out, and I've been meditating for a pretty long time. I wish I could just take an FDA-approved "Buddhism Pill" one morning, wait a half-hour, and then never have any more cravings for material items—and no more guilt, either. Of course, if there were such a pill it would quickly get branded by a "Buddhist" pharmaceutical company, mass-produced, and endorsed by Buddhist celebrities. Before long we'd all be addicted to it. Truthfully, it's great that there is no way to annihilate desire. The moment of WANT is really the misunderstood urge to connect with the world around us.

What Buddhist meditation offers is a group of techniques to deal sanely and effectively with the moments of WANT, as they arise in the mind of an individual. These techniques generally involve resting with the impulse of craving long enough to gain some insight into how it functions. Without that awareness, we become flimsy puppets to our consumeristic mentality, susceptible to endless manipulations of our desires, both external and internal. It's fascinating that American political rhetoric often equates the privilege of our country's democratic freedoms with the ability to consume freely. But being a hungry ghost isn't any kind of freedom I'd like to have.

Of course, consumerism runs deep and the impulses that fuel it are complex. Contemporary advertising has become very good at using our awareness of the postmodern irony of our own consumption and desires. A 2006 Sprite campaign called "Sublymonal Advertising" plays off our wariness of subliminal messages, using that wariness as the very basis of its selling point. It's an art piece—almost—a self-critique of advertising, but with an artificially flavored twist. The audience is meant to notice—not ignore as usual—the meaninglessness of choosing one type of high fructose corn syrup over another. The campaign ends with a not-so-subtle message to the consumer: "OBEY," and then jumps quickly to an image of a can of Sprite.

It's a new type of ad—the "obviously subliminal" message. The ad almost says: "You know all our tricks already. We know you know them. But here's the thing: You know you have no idea how to deal with craving. You know that we know you have no idea how to deal with craving. So drink Sprite." The ad tauntingly calls full attention to advertising's power over us. The one thing that such an ad can never meaningfully call our attention to, however, is the hollow nature of *WANT* itself. Because *that* would invariably lessen the amount of Sprite we drink.

Often we make consumption choices because we fall prey to a blasé "Whatever." We know, as we pull out the credit card, that we're caving to empty longings. But we do it anyway, and maybe like that Sprite spot suggests, we celebrate the irony of the no-longer-hidden meaninglessness of our choices. Saying "whatever," obeying, gives us the permission to celebrate the insubstantiality of our decisions. But that "whatever" mind is really just laziness. We don't allow ourselves to believe that we can actually over-come our hungry-ghost mentality. But we *can*—we just might not know how yet.

In my own experience, the moment of WANT—fiery, grinding, and all-consuming as it may feel—is always also intangible and ethereal. I can't ever quite pin the tail on the craving. No matter what object I think I want, the *WA*NT itself never has any real essence. The hungry ghost is always just a shadow puppet, no matter how real he seems or how much he seems to be pulling all my strings. Seeing this is the key to becoming a more responsible consumer: we can begin to move through the world in a way that nei-ther denies ourselves enjoyment, nor claims too much for ourselves.

It doesn't help to be wracked with guilt about the legit-imacy of your own existence. It's good to have a sense of humor about your relative wealth, your opportunities, and your habits. We need to take enough time to consistently investigate the effects of our consumption choices. Gather-ing information on responsible consumption is not the easiest thing to do, even when we feel inspired to do it. We may never be able to make consumption choices that cause zero harm, but we can always make choices that cause *less* harm. It takes more time and energy, but that energy is made available to us when we witness the transparency of our *WA*NT.

WHAT WOULD AN ECONOMICS OF GENEROSITY look like? Maybe not that different from our current sys-tem, except that the mentality that drives individuals' choices would be oriented in a new direction. What if each individual who made up our system of economic interactions operated on this basic principle: "Each time this wheel of fortune goes around, each time I engage in an economic exchange, let me put in slightly more than I take out. Let my actions maximize the welfare of those around me." This is the intuitive mental formula of free-market generosity. With it, even the most barren desert can develop into a lush, abundant garden. If we contribute to shared resources more than we extract, our garden will always be sustainable. This isn't a utopian vision or a John Lennon song—it's common sense, even if it's not so common in our current system.

One thing is certain: if less of our material and psychic energy goes to ourselves, and more goes to others, that basic shift will make a huge impact in the network of interdependence. When we contemplate our consumption this way, the battle of practicing generosity is already half-won. Interestingly enough, practicing generosity can also be a great way to flip the script on our hungry-ghost mentality, to convert the moment of *WANT* into a moment of offering.

THERE IS ENOUGH. There is always enough for us. Our mind is a self-sustaining garden. The world has plenty of resources to support us. We don't need to pillage and plunder for fleeting fixes. Desire is nothing to avoid—it is the magnetic force that connects us to others, but we can't let it run amok. We can actually come to need *less*. And when we need less, we will have MORE to offer. It is *actually that simple.*

THE OTHER SIDE of generosity's coin is offering. Systematically practicing offering does two things. First, it benefits the mind of the person who offers, by relaxing the hungry-ghost reflex, the spastic need to indulge a fleeting fix whenever a moment of WANT arises. Second, it helps those receiving the offering by sustaining and supporting them. This also creates a crucial awareness of the interconnection between giver and receiver in any transaction.

Despite these positive effects, offering can be difficult. Our acts of generosity are often not well received; we are left "uncredited" for our gesture. You clean your whole apartment and your roommate doesn't even notice. You give money to a disaster relief organization only to find out that—thanks to an obnoxious level of bureaucracy— the money never reached the people it was meant for. You take a half-hour to separate all the recycling only to watch one careless sanitation worker throw it in with the rest of the trash.

The first rule of offering is simple: *Don't ever expect anyone else to notice.** Of course, people will sometimes notice and thank us for our generosity, but not always at the time or place of our choosing, and almost never in the exact way we'd expect. (A life lived *practicing* offering will almost certainly result in a larger crowd at your funeral service, if that's any incentive.) But even when no one else is paying attention to our actions, offering still has its biggest payoff on the level of interdependence of the self, because it transforms our inner hungry ghost into a decent, low-maintenance human being.

The first practice of offering is giving material things and energetic effort to others. On the level of relationships, this means giving what your friends and family need. On the level of community and society, this means being a responsible citizen, volunteering, and donating your time

*THIS RULE SUCKS.

and money to the causes and people with which you connect. Public workers rarely get thanked for their efforts maintaining the vast infrastructure of our communities. Practicing offering could be as easy as delivering two unexpected words to them. Or, instead of spending $20 on dinner at a restaurant, at least occasionally consider spending 7 bucks making dinner, and giving the other $13 to someone who needs it more. We can always do something.

On a deeper level, the practice of offering goes beyond the gift of any particular object. The act of offering develops into offering our very *presence* as our gift to no one in particular. To everyone. The way our presence ripples out into the network of interdependence is often invisible. But it's felt; it's real.

I've always been astounded by the potency of an individual's presence. Presence may not be quantifiable, but there's no doubting its tangible aura. It's this power of an individual's presence that has been perverted and morphed into our strange celebrity culture. The existence of celebrities—as morbid as the tabloids and magazines often seem—points to something deeply human. Every culture on Earth has its famous people. Celebrities wouldn't exist if individuals didn't naturally possess the power and charm to turn other people's heads. A person holding the space of generosity can actually change the atmosphere of a room, the feel of a city, even the momentum of a civilization. This level of generosity allows us to become natural leaders, empowered not by any formal governing body, but by our presence itself.

One of my best friends made an inspiring documentary called *Favela Rising*. It's the story of a musician in the slums of Rio de Janeiro, one of the most violent cities on Earth. This musician, Anderson Sá, began running music workshops in the 1990s to get kids into music-making and away from involvement in the drug armies that control the squatter settlements of Rio. Anderson's movement has led to thousands of kids becoming members of music workshops instead of drug dealers. As the story develops, the basic reason that Anderson's movement is successful becomes crystal clear. It's not so much that music is cooler than drugs. It's that *Anderson* is cooler than the drug dealers. He is tremendously endearing with a great smiling presence that radiates contentment with himself. His presence itself is an offering that spreads out in all directions. Whenever I meet somebody like that, whose continuous gift is her very presence, I always think to myself: "I'll have what she's having."

We need to use our very presence to begin to demonstrate—not through words but through personal manifestation—that being a kind, considerate, creative person is more fashionable, more in demand, and just plain better than being self-absorbed. By doing this, we are rising up against our own habitual malaise, and the engrained communal tendencies of our culture. This kind of inner shift is capable of transforming a human being into a kind of walking message that says: "I'm proof there's a way to be content and fulfilled without screwing other people." Our presence proclaims that there's a way to live more simply. There's a way to recycle your human energy for the benefit of others. And *you* will be better off for it.

In Buddhism, the highest level of generosity is called giving the gift of dharma, the gift of truth. This practice hinges on the old saying: "Give a man a fish and he'll eat for a day. Teach him to fish and he'll eat forever." We can teach a person to "eat forever" by giving a path of wisdom to someone else. This means teaching, but that definitely doesn't only mean engaging in formal teaching or spiritual teaching. As part of our practice of offering, we could commit to at least one ongoing relationship in our life where we are guiding somebody else along a path to her or his own fulfillment and understanding. This could mean mentoring, this could mean babysitting, this could even mean teaching glassblowing or coaching Little League.

There is no person with more potential to affect the network of interdependence than a teacher. In the absence of good teaching and mentorship, all kinds of bad things can happen. In their *presence*, people develop and flourish along their own trajectory, learning how to fish in the deepest sense of the metaphor.

It's incredible how teachers are treated in our society. A basketball player makes more money in one day than a good schoolteacher makes in a year, and we accept this as a "natural" and normal outcome of the market. Why don't we as individuals make the choice to reciprocate the generosity of those who manifest as teachers in our own life, instead of buying tickets to next week's game?

There are many ways you can practice offering, and there are specific Buddhist meditation practices for developing our own practice of offering. The basic premise is that by consistently resting with the arising of our cravings, our own seeming need to consume, we begin to need less. By needing less, we simply have more to offer.

What and how we offer is ultimately up to us.

CHAPTER 6:
ENTERTAINMENT AIN'T
SO ENTERTAINING

The Earth is not a flatscreen.

SAUL WILLIAMS

HAVE YOU EVER FOUND YOURSELF WATCHING a YouTube video while listening to your iPod while sending one person a text message from your phone and another person an email and a third an instant message from your computer, all while trying to talk to a fourth person on your land line—as you munch away at a bag of chips? Yeah, me too.

I like to pretend it's a way to accomplish more with my limited supplies of time and energy. I even give it a long name to make it sound important and efficient: "multitasking." What I'm really doing is drowning out the fidgets of boredom, stretching out those octopus tentacles of distraction, and not really accomplishing any of the actual tasks on my to-do list. Being able to do more than one thing in general is, of course, wonderful; it's a mark of versatility, flexibility of mind, diversity of interests. Doing more than one thing *at a time*, however, is not so great.

The line between entertainment and everything else keeps getting blurrier, and the entertainment itself is getting more and more intricate and compelling. Online, we can already live a mostly virtual life, although at this point the interface is still a screen in front of us. We're probably not far from a time when a complete home entertainment system is a microchip implanted in the human skull, capable of projecting any desired imagescape or ambient soundtrack into the sensory regions of our brain, letting us freefall into an alternate reality for days at a time. The remote control for this system could easily be thought-activated; a bored twitch of mindlessness could change the "channel," and then the ambient environment would shift to accommodate the whim of the thought-activated fantasy. Maybe this new implanted system will be branded with a name like "Zen 3000," "Namasté," or maybe even the "EnlightenPod."

The number of bits of information that enter our brain each second now is truly staggering, and the volume keeps increasing as bandwidths broaden. This increase has caused profound changes in the way we interact with our sense perceptions. Computer screens usually have multiple windows open at once—widgets, news tickers, and feeds flying all over the place. TVs and movie screens have streaming text, split screens, those giant ads that pop up in the corners—right at the best parts. Are we ever looking at just one thing? We're certainly almost never *doing* just one thing— except when we sleep.

Mine was the first generation of Americans to grow up with video games and home computers. Apparently, we haven't grown up all that much. In fact, the *average age* of an avid video game player in America is now twenty-nine, according to a 2004 NPR survey. That's right, twenty-nine.

The other day I was excited that a large group of people showed up at a meditation gathering, until I walked down the block to see twenty times as many people—no kids among them—camped out overnight in front of an electronics store waiting with almost religious resolve to buy the new PlayStation! The worldwide video game industry was valued at approximately $30 billion in 2006, several times the value of the Hollywood movie industry. On top of all that, the next generation now has iPhones, WiFi, and text messaging. These objects have *a very real* effect on the way we focus our attention, develop our awareness, and interface with everything around us. They change the way we handle ourselves. They alter our basic methods of communication and socialization. They rearrange our very conception of space and time.

In many ways, this is all a blessing. Our increased ability to do more than one thing at a time, our increasing modes of available communication, and the hyberbolically increasing coolness of entertainment are genuine triumphs of modern technology. I constantly marvel at the various technological means we have to connect with each other. Most of us (except for the true hermits, yogis, and Luddites out there) probably have more friends and know more people than we would've been able to ten years ago, just because of communication technology. Where we used to write a hundred letters or make a hundred phone calls, we can now send a quick email with a hundred cc's, or a two-line text message. On the bright side of interdependence, the fact that we have all of our gadgets definitely seems to help bring people together.

On the darker side, there is a great deal about (a) our quest to be relentlessly entertained, and (b) our need to do many different things at once, that causes problems. Through their baffling powers of disconnection, entertainment and multitasking both put us on a not-so-magic carpet ride that carries us far away from recognition of interdependence. It takes a ton of discipline not to be taken on this ride.

BUDDHISM'S DEFINITION OF DISCIPLINE is that we consciously bind ourselves to a code of conduct. Not because we absolutely believe in right or wrong, or in some objectively determined good and bad. Such black and white distinctions don't ultimately hold up on the level of universal interdependence of all concepts. The rules for how we carry ourselves are not written on stone tablets and brought down from the mountain by some Buddhist Charlton Heston. Regulations do not descend from some authority on high. If a teacher or someone we trust tells us to do something, we might be wise to heed them, but in my experience, meaningful discipline rarely comes from an outer authority. As a teenager I loved to read, but as soon as it became a required homework assignment, all joy was sucked out of the endeavor.

We develop a personal code of conduct because we start to see—for ourselves—that some activities lead us to feeling fulfilled, productive, creative, and whole while others make us feel cut-off, isolated, fidgety, addicted, and generally worthless—to ourselves and the people around us. Practicing discipline means that, for our own benefit, we create a code of conduct, a means of staying connected to our own ripening wisdom about what to do and what to avoid.

In Buddhism, discipline is formally encapsulated in taking vows. With a vow, we make a spoken commitment to work with our destructive habits. Many of us think that taking a vow means we guarantee never to do something again. But anyone who has that super-heroic ability to restrain themselves probably doesn't need to take a vow in the first place.

Taking a vow is not offering our personal guarantees of perfection. It is much more practical than that. When we take a vow, we know, from the beginning, that we will break it—and probably pretty often. The formal Buddhist vows are designed that way. We can stray a long way from the home base of our commitment, but at a certain point the recollection of the promise you made snaps back, bungee-like, and you're brought back to the path with elastic force. The vows function as reminders to deal with our anger, our laziness, our selfishness, and all our damaging habits. This kind of discipline reminds us of the most basic lesson of interdependence: *what we do matters*. A vow continually taps us on the shoulder, saying, "Remember me? I'm Awareness, and that cat over there is called Compassion, and you promised to spend more time with us. How you doing?" These vows are each a beacon of discipline, a homing device when the proverbial forest is invisible through the trees.

The discipline that leads to an intelligent and non-oppressive code of conduct comes from beginning to witness the functioning of habit. We develop firsthand awareness of all the things we do that take us away from meaningful living. At the time of the historical Buddha, his community took vows not to consume intoxicating substances, for instance, but not because there was something inherently evil about beer. Rather, he and his monks agreed that being too hungover to meditate would be a bad thing.

Meditation was their most meaningful way to spend time. If they hadn't personally understood the painful consequences of drinking alcohol (a hangover), the monks probably would've rebelled against the Buddha's code. Then, the Buddha might have considered employing some kind of deceptive propaganda, sermonizing with fearsome fire-and-brimstone to get the monks to obey. But rules based on propaganda or the threat of external force always crumble under their own hypocrisy eventually. Commitments that come from within tend to be much more durable and long-lasting, because their importance is self-realized and self-sustaining.

For those of us who are twenty-nine or thirty or even forty and still addicted to PlayStation or Xbox, Buddhism is not telling us to give up the video game because video games are inherently mindless. There are stories of ancient practitioners becoming enlightened just by sweeping the floor again and again; with the right intention and viewpoint, a person could probably even become enlightened by playing Vice City. It's unlikely, though.

What Buddhism might say about these games is more like this: "If you have found, honestly in your own experience, that you're addicted to your controller and glued to the screen for six hours a day, and it turns you into a drooling zombie with zero friends, no job, and no relationship, and you feel like you're wasting your life pretending to be a virtual Jedi made out of digitized bytes and pixels, and all your real-life clothes are stained with pizza sauce, and you don't have any voice messages from people you care about, and you haven't been out of your house yet this week except to buy Ramen noodles and toilet paper, and all of these facts *actually bother you*, instead of just hitting that reset button again, you might want to develop the discipline to do something more fulfilling with your time." (If video games are not your thing, insert personal poison above.)

If our habits don't bother us, then there really isn't any point in practicing discipline, no reason to even contemplate crafting a code of self-conduct. Discipline is about limiting the harm done to our own mind and making choices that create a supportive environment for our development. Then we can also create supportive environments for the people around us.

Guilt is not a part of this kind of discipline's package deal. Guilt about our bad habits doesn't help at all. Guilt usually entrenches a habit more deeply—popping pimple after pimple only to see your face become scarred. Having good discipline requires replacing guilt with the growing confidence that there is a natural intelligence in us somewhere, a self-awareness of our positive and negative tendencies. It's pretty amazing that we have our own internal radar of what is beneficial and what is harmful—and if we start listening to it we see it's actually reliable. Meditation helps us learn what is creative and what is destructive in our experience. Discipline is about learning to be a good draftsman who draws fine lines in the shifting sand of our habits. The challenge is holding ourselves to the lines we draw even though we know they're not unchanging and absolute truths, and not caving in to our laziness every time a little resistance strikes.

Sometimes our habits can be incredibly subtle and far below the threshold of awareness, and it takes a long while before we even notice that we might be doing something destructive. Yet often a destructive tendency is very clear and painfully obvious to us and everyone else—but we do it anyway. (I don't think that crack addicts would claim smoking crack is somehow "good for you," for example.)

As practitioners, we have to become deeply familiar with the canyon-sized grooves of our habits before they ever start to change. Sometimes I have to mindfully watch myself fall into the damaging rut of a particular habit around twenty million times before I begin to not crash into it so easily. When our habits are less obvious, it's even trickier, because it's so hard to see if we're caught up in something harmful or just enjoying ourselves. The harder it is to see a fine line, the easier it becomes to justify that there's no line at all.

WE ALL NEED TIME TO RELAX. Sometimes your brain just gets fried like a sweet plantain. We all have our escapes. We all have those little things (or big things) we do to escape the blunt and sometimes harsh toil of this present moment: coffee, cigarettes, marijuana (which we called "Buddha" as kids in New York), MySpacing, websurfing, popcorn-eating, DVD-renting, reality TV–watching, nose-picking—on and on and on.

We're a society of entertainment junkies, hooked from birth, individually and collectively, fed the sugar-high dazzle of entertainment through an intravenous cable tube. And the cruelest joke of any bad habit is that when you're hooked, you don't really even enjoy the fix anymore.

Any escape can rapidly morph into a vicious addiction. We might not even notice we're addicted to something until the fix is taken away from us. As an experiment, if you normally surf the Internet and check your email multiple times every day, try not going online at all for just three days. Call it an Internet Cleanse. Commit to it and see how you feel during and after the experiment.

When we're addicted to anything, whatever it is, we wrap our minds up in a thick haze, unable to ever find real rest in the present moment. The strength of the addiction and the density of the haze seem to be directly related. Within a mind that needs to constantly escape, the prospect of boredom is the worst nightmare. Boredom is the most obvious symptom of withdrawal from the fix of entertainment. This withdrawal symptom is why meditation is often so difficult. And so powerful.

When we get bored meditating, we can't really blame it on anyone else, because we're sitting there alone with our own mind. We're actually addicted to the fundamental escape of *never wanting to be alone with ourselves*. This is a tough fact to face, but you confront it repeatedly in meditation practice. Meditation might be the only period of time in a day when you are both awake and completely unplugged. The only home entertainment center left is the mind itself.

When we practice, we catch on pretty quick that our usual m.o. is always *needing an entertainment fix and needing it right now*: another drink, another puff, another flick of the remote, another click that opens an already bookmarked page in the same old browser, yet another empty download. Many people I know—myself included—have destroyed ourselves in ways small and large, just to avoid the realization that we're unbearably sick of seeing that same old face in the mirror.

The pain of knowing that we're not actually doing things that fulfill us can drive us to develop some pretty intricate and brilliant mechanisms to justify our escapes into entertainment. One justification is to constantly shift the opportunity to do meaningful things to an imaginary future place and time. (This is a very fancy way of saying *procrastination*.)

Or, how about the witty nihilism of convincing ourselves that how we spend our time doesn't *really* matter at all? Wouldn't that make everything so much easier, if cause and effect lived galaxies away from each other? Maybe we could even manipulate our understanding of the universal interdependence of all ideas. We could say that any notions of "creative" and "destructive" or positive and negative habits are *just clichéd value judgments*. The idea that there's really such a thing as helpful and harmful habits is just a culturally relative notion that somebody pulled out of a hat because they had nothing better to do with their time, right? Once again, this is the "Whatever" mentality in all its glory. As if our very existence could be summarized with an ironic shrug of the shoulders and an apathetic laugh.

Having the discipline to stay present with interdependence doesn't mean there's no joy, no time to relax, no fun. There's a very subtle and elusive line that no one else can find for us; we have to draw it ourselves. It's the line between enjoying oneself and being addicted to escapes, between appreciating real creativity and witnessing the subtle damage of entertainment. And just to be clear: a path with no joy is nihilism, not Buddhism.

Seeing what's wrong with entertainment doesn't mean that you give up your art. In my experience, it's the exact opposite; meditation actually deepens the potency of the creative process. There is a subtle difference in the way the mind engages in art and the way it engages in entertainment, a fine line between cultural exploration and blind escape. There's a difference between enjoying a well-crafted film and watching a bad one that you've already seen four times. The difference is in the way your mind engages in those two activities. The mind that needs to be entertained hunts for modes of engagement that sedate it, rendering it dull and numb. And once we're tranquilized this way, our reality becomes little more than a giant cocoon of ambient experience.

Art, on the other hand, should challenge us to be aware and alive; it should require us to be present and accounted for during the journey. Art is another way to bring us into the naked awe of our own minds' interaction with experience. Entertainment is how we avoid that challenge. Practicing an art form is without a doubt a practice of interdependence, because we are giving the gift of expression to the communities we inhabit.

LET'S FACE IT, we all live busy lives and we need all the help we can get to accomplish everything we want to do. So, what's the problem with multitasking? Its logic is pretty straightforward: we work hard, usually too hard. The more chores we can do simultaneously, the more time there is to enjoy the things that really matter—friends, family, creative pursuits, relaxation. If we can get more than one thing done at a time, why don't we just go ahead and do it, and kill a few birds with one Blackberry?

This is the myth of multitasking. The myth of multitasking is crafted around a very convincing argument for efficiency and effectiveness. If we can multitask more and more, we assume, then we will have more time and availability for the people and things that matter to us. The logic makes total sense.

Unfortunately, a human being is not built like an octopus, and multitasking is just not very conducive to the design of the human mind. Scientific studies have already exposed the mistaken assertion that multitasking is a more efficient way of getting things done. According to a meditator's understanding of how mindfulness and awareness operate and develop in the mind, the problem with multitasking is simple: if we have too many objects for our mindfulness to keep track of at one time, our mind can't deepen its familiarity with any of them. With too many points of focus, the mind can't really immerse itself in each object's function beyond the realm of superficial glances. If our attention is split-screened, our mindfulness has to leapfrog around to assemble a coherent picture. And when we leapfrog from object to object, task to task, we only delve halfheartedly into each of the particular objects of our attention.

It's only when our attention can rest on an object or a task for a little while that we can activate our natural intelligence and deepen our comprehension of the object or task at hand. And it's only when we deepen familiarity that we can actually become effective at performing the task with insight and intelligence. For example, if I'm talking on the phone, drinking a beer, cooking soup, and listening to music all at once, what will happen? In my experience, chances are the soup will burn, I won't know if I'm drinking a pilsner or a lager, I'm not going to really hear what the person I'm talking with is saying, and I won't even recognize the notes or the beats of the music. I set out to have four simultaneously meaningful experiences, I end up with zero.

Multitasking is also all about avoiding boredom. It's a bedtime story we tell ourselves before we fall asleep to interdependence. Resting your mind on one object at a time can be incredibly boring. The simplicity of just cooking soup without music or cell phone means that I actually have to watch the soup and only the soup. That's boring. But thankfully, it can also be incredibly beautiful, not to mention leading to good soup.

When we try to do more than one thing at a time, another deeper problem starts to develop. In the frenzy of juggling it all, we tend to shift our focus away from the things that matter and toward activities we don't really *need* to be doing at all. We add unnecessary tasks to our to-do list, dive into them, and lose touch with priorities. What begins with the best intentions—to get more meaningful things accomplished—turns into a roadrunner cyclone of mental wind. We never get right to the point. It's so easy to fall into this trap—especially if you live in a big city where there is always a lot going on.

The truth is, the important things in life aren't very easy to actually *do*. Somehow, we're tremendously resistant to doing the very things we have ourselves determined to be priorities. We try to take the edge off the scary boredom of that simplicity by concocting both the need and ability to do other things at the same time. If we want to truly accomplish many things in our life, then we need to try to do one thing at a time. That might be the best five-syllable mantra ever: *one thing at a time*. Cook soup when you're cooking soup. Write an email when you're writing an email. Listen to Stevie Wonder when you are listening to Stevie Wonder. After all, Stevie deserves your undivided attention.

THE TRUE THREAT posed by entertainment and multitasking is that they always cause our minds to move in one direction—away from other people and the world in which we live. Our minds don't spin off into outer space;

they spin off into inner space. Entertainment, escapes, and addictions make us fundamentally unavailable to ourselves, unavailable to our friends, unavailable in our communities, and unavailable to the world—like a big DO NOT DISTURB sign hanging prominently around our neck. At the same time, a mind that multitasks is also less available to others, no matter how much we try to convince ourselves that the opposite is true. After all, when we're constantly juggling, our hands are never free for a good hug.

Thinking about other people can be incredibly helpful to the path of our own discipline. That might sound a little selfish, and maybe it is, but in a positive way. For example, when I remember that people might read this book and possibly get something meaningful for themselves out of it, it makes it much easier to turn off the Battlestar Galactica DVD and get back to the writing. If I thought I was only writing this for myself alone, I might convince myself to watch just one more episode right now (just one). But then in my mind I see your unknown face, whoever you might be, in the vast network of interdependence. With that vision, I turn off the DVD and snap back to my writing practice, clicked back into place by the elastic memory of my commitment.

We can use our desire to connect with other people as the inspiration to gently take our personal discipline up a notch. We can be confident that our positive actions have an effect on others and that our destructive habits keep us isolated and frozen. This confidence is the bungee-cord of awareness—our implicit (or explicit) vow to get and stay connected. The more we envision and construct the important things in our life in terms of our connection with and dependence on others, the smaller and smaller our bad habits will seem in comparison.

DISCIPLINE DOESN'T MEAN LIMITING your freedom. It's the impetus for developing a structure to your activity, which comes from taking deadly seriously—with a strong sense of humor—the truth of interdependence.

CHAPTER 7:
NONVIOLENCE OR NONEXISTENCE

Men, for years now, have been talking about war
and peace. But now, no longer can they just talk
about it. It is no longer a choice between violence
and nonviolence in this world; it's nonviolence or
nonexistence.

DR. MARTIN LUTHER KING, JR.

(the day before he was assassinated)

THE CONNECTION BETWEEN NONVIOLENCE
and interdependence is crucial. When the nature of anger is
misunderstood, no mental force can take us away from the
truth of interdependence more swiftly. Violence makes us fall
into grotesque and primal misconceptions of separation. The
growl of aggression sucks us from the realm of human decency down into a hellish zone of Us-*versus*-Them, and me-
against-the-world mentalities. The bitter mind-frame of
violence is ancient, engrained in our evolution since the first
two amoebae battled over a tiny glob of protein.

For thousands of years our human cultures have been utterly dysfunctional about the relationship between aggression and peace. The twentieth century was almost a hundred straight years of wars among empires of hungry ghosts, viciously addicted to the fleeting economic fix of creating new enemies. Each war carried a surprisingly similar rhetoric of xenophobia. And each time, violence was presented as the necessary precursor for a true and lasting peace. We were always fighting in the present so, somehow, we wouldn't have to fight in the future; fighting them over there so we wouldn't have to fight them over here, and on and on. Each time the rhetorical future became the actual present and then the textbook past, the cycle proved to be both endless and fruitless. The twenty-first century is picking up right where the twentieth left off, with better weapons. There's only one little problem with the logic of violence: war doesn't end war—any more than a heroin fix ends a heroin addiction.

Could you imagine an action hero whose greatest power was systematically conquering his own aggression? How would the camera pick up the subtleties of a struggle without a definable external enemy? How would an action movie even begin to convey the narrative of an inner conquest of aggression? Can you imagine Gandhi softly uttering some Schwarzenegger-like catchphrase as he sat there mindfully and took a beating from the British army? Yet, in terms of interdependence, Gandhi makes Schwarzenegger's heroes look like so-called "girly-men" every day of the week.

In the history of the twentieth century, in each of the rare moments that nonviolence was practiced by a broad, inclusive, and focused group of people, it achieved more beneficial results for the society in question than were achieved by any war in the same century.

The devil's advocate will probably bring up Hitler (or Hitleresque figures) as a prime example of the occasional need for violence and say that the world would be an awful place if we didn't take him out. But the devil's advocate misses the deepest layer of interdependence in the Hitler example, which is this: *the machinery of violence is what brought Hitler to power.* If there had been a broad-based, strong, and fearless movement toward nonviolence in Germany around 1920, there would never have been a powerful Hitler, because the interdependent causes and conditions necessary to bring him to power would never have come to be.

Every argument that violence is necessary falls into the trap of viewing cause and effect only in the short term, at a time when the reactive crisis has already arisen. Arguments for pre-emption and even many arguments for self-defense are only short-term solutions which repeatedly miss the long scope of interdependence's sight.

The reason that nonviolence is always much more powerful than violence is simple: nonviolence arises from a mind that understands the way interdependence actually works, the true functioning of cause and effect. Violence arises from a mind that doesn't. The long-term ripple effects of violence *always* reverberate back to the aggressor in awful and unexpected ways. This is primarily because our own aggressive tendencies condition and habituate our own minds towards "resolving" conflict in the same way in the future. Which means we keep finding ourselves magically surrounded by thugs the next time around, and the one after that too, and we find ourselves saying: "Well, I have to protect myself" all over again. This is the collective mindset that creates the military-industrial complex. Yes, the violence of World War II put an end to Hitler. But the violence of World War II did not put an end to violence—the episodes of that tired plotline resumed only a few short years later. Only nonviolence can end war.

THE PRACTICE OF INTERDEPENDENCE constantly brings us back from the theories of the societal level down to the finer level of individual actions. Violence is not just about the workings of some vague and massive military-industrial complex, and it doesn't always come equipped with night-vision goggles, desert tanks, high-tech rifles, or terrorists' dirty bombs. Violence is right here in our bodies and minds, hatched from an icy glance, spiteful words, or bitter thoughts detonated quietly on inner minefields. Violence is a confused reaction to the inevitable arising of anger within the space of an individual's mind.

Anger is not violence in and of itself—there needs to be a distinction between these two words. Sometimes, when we start thinking about spiritual ideals, we tend to mistake any moment of anger for the deep confusion of violence. In some haloed notion of sanctity, we think that just by getting mad we're doing something horribly wrong. "If I were a good meditator, a good Buddhist prac-titioner, a good spiritual person, I wouldn't be mad right now." Then you get mad at yourself for getting angry. Finally you get even madder at yourself for failing to rec-ognize the obvious Buddhist irony of getting angry at yourself for getting angry. And now you got a good old triple-layer cake of anger, frustration, and self-loathing.

So we try to make amends by resolving to speak in hushed humble tones from now onward, and affecting the air of a quiet saint, hoping that no one ever gets the impres-sion that we're trying to assert anything forcefully. We stencil

W-E-L-C-O-M-E on our own foreheads, transforming our-selves into doormats for other people because we think we're supposed to be passive at all costs. We suppress any irritation beneath a game-show smile, and aspire to never find fault with anyone or anything, aiming for some blissfully passive-aggressive "It's-All-Good" state where anger has been pushed back into our pores forever. And we desperately hope everyone else can witness the depths of our "equanimity."

But this isn't what anger is all about, and we shouldn't be too quick to dismiss its potency. Anger contains a great deal of wisdom, especially the wisdom to know what is wrong, both within us and around us. Anger is also the nec-essary inspirational fuel for changing any negative situation into a more positive one. When it comes through with set-tled clarity, anger says "You know what? Something is WRONG here. This is not the way to treat people. This is not what good political leadership looks like. This is not the world I want to live in!" Anger is what gets us off our asses and drives us toward transformative action.

There's a bumper sticker that says, "If you're not out-raged, you're not paying attention." Anyone who never gets angry when he sees their friends and loved ones doing things that are harmful to themselves or others has to be pretty numb to the deep sadness of suffering. Anyone who just walks on by when she sees humans being treated like objects needs to take a second look. And a third one.

It can even be helpful to get angry at our own shortcom-ings if we can do it without falling into that bottomless crater of guilt and inadequacy. Anger smacks us forcefully and exposes our tendency to glaze over and ignore our individ-ual and collective problems. When we see something wrong, something ignorant, something oppressive, it's a mark of natural intelligence and sensitivity that we would get angry, *especially* when we are committed to investigating the causal web that connects people and events together. Anger is so powerful, it's *nuclear*. Like any power source, it can be deadly if not handled properly, and helpful if used skillfully. If we misuse anger we can fall prey to the destructiveness of violence. Violence is what happens when anger is misunderstood. Intelligence and transformative action are what manifest when anger is seen clearly and utilized properly.

One of my favorite lines in Buddhist teaching says, "If you have not tamed the enemy of your own hatred, then combating outer opponents will only make them multiply." That says it all. Hatred and violence ignore the truth of interdependence on a fundamental level. This ignorance arises because the logic of violence always causes us to construct a false us/them dichotomy, ignoring interdependence. Any time we do that, bad things are bound to happen. We go to war to have fewer enemies, and we always, always end up with more. Every time.

This statement about taming our own anger has direct implications for anyone involved in any kind of activism. When you get involved in any cause, there needs to be some anger in you, because otherwise your fuel tank for action will be running on empty. You won't have much to give to your cause. The danger of activism, in terms of interdependence, lies in the problem of anchoring our righteous cause in opposition to a set enemy, a fixed group of antagonists whose image we can imprint in our brain and forever burn in effigy.

The more we fix our identity around the evil of a given enemy, "them," the less chance there will be to ever meaningfully dissolve that dichotomy. In other words, if we don't tame our own anger, we will become addicted to framing everything in those terms, "us" and "them." When that happens, the needed fix for the addiction is in finding new enemies. This is how our inner military-industrial complex builds its own artillery. Once we need a new enemy, we can easily create the mental propaganda that explains why some new person or group or regime fits the bill. Finding the reason why our enemy is our enemy just takes a good Orwellian storyteller and decent production values.

When we fall into this rut, we will have less and less reason for an actual resolution to the conflict in question. Because if the people I've defined as my enemies for so long stop being the "them" on which I've been fixating, then I will have to stop being part of the "us" to which I've grown so accustomed. Once you've been protesting for a while, it can be truly scary to have to face losing your identity as the "protestor." If fighting is what we're addicted to, there will always be someone to fight (isn't it funny how enemies just seem to keep on coming, and coming, and coming?). It might be exes or bosses. It might be Republicans or Democrats. It might be Iranians or Chinese, or the world's most irresponsible corporations—but we'll always be in need of and be able to find an enemy, a "them." And when our anger turns to violence, we'll be blessed by more enemies than we could ever imagine.

One of the most helpful issues that Buddhism addresses is the very simple fact that while our anger is often (but not always) directed externally, anger itself always resides internally, in the mind of the one who feels it and acts upon it. This is a crucial point: our general tendency in the moment of anger is to shift our focus to the object of the anger, instead of the subject who is feeling it.

We often ignore the hidden, inner effects of violence on the individual who feels it. The purveyor of violence always hurts himself before he hurts anyone else. When we're caught in anger, our thoughts operate like tiny machetes. Most of the time, all that results from our rage is that we hack our insides to pieces. This is the first level that we must face violence on, the level of the self. And of course, when we fall into self-violence, becoming both the subject and the object of the feeling, those machetes cut us even more deeply.

We shouldn't underestimate the amount of damage that violence does on this level alone, even when our anger feels completely intelligent and fully justified. As a personal example, there is a certain world leader who has constantly brought anger boiling to the surface in me, since the very start of this twenty-first century. But honestly, when I think about all of the moments I tormented myself with inner violence toward this iconic figure, I arrive at the following personal insight: Any harm he has caused me has been immensely compounded by the harm I've caused myself, hacking myself to pieces with hatred toward him.

VERY FEW OF US have received adequate training in dealing with the moments of our own anger. Fortunately, this is precisely the kind of training that practicing meditation provides. The thing about anger is that it hurts. It hurts bad, much worse than we often want to admit, which is why we don't want to deal with it. It's palpable, uncomfortable— a craggy meteorite crashing inside our ribcage. There's nothing subtle about the feeling—it's deeply physical. It's hard to simply let ourselves be uncomfortable that way, to simply rest with, be present with—and even embody—the tangible sensations that anger unleashes. Part of the reason that the mistake of violence is made at all is that we just don't know how to dwell in discomfort without some rebellion against the perceived source of our pain. But you have to get used to discomfort if you're going to have any chance to practice nonviolence. In fact, you have to get used to discomfort if you want to be a living being.

Let's face it: a lot of the circumstances that make us angry on a daily basis are truly petty, often to the point of comedy. If something happens to take us even an inch outside of our comfort zone, we freak out, like the apocalypse is nigh. My good friend was working at a Starbucks in one of the wealthiest neighborhoods in New York. Eventually he had to quit, because so many customers drove him crazy with tiny issues they had with their orders of extra-foam mochaccinos with soymilk and 1.5 Splendas. He was continually accosted about the minute imperfections of lattés. He couldn't absorb the petty violence anymore, so he quit. Nobody wants to feel worthless like that, nobody wants to feel like a grande-sized indentured servant. That's what petty violence does to the people who have to receive it.

Of course, maybe you don't fall into the specific trap of getting angry this way. Maybe you don't create this kind of "latté suffering." Even if you're easily satisfied by a seventy-five-cent cup of sludgy deli coffee, or by no coffee at all, you must have something petty in your life that upsets you, something that you know is a little bit ridiculous for you to get angry about. And our inability to deal with the petty discomfort of the petty stuff that angers us makes us behave

in a way that's . . . well . . . *petty*. And then we react by causing (more than) petty suffering to ourselves and others.
Think of all the thousands and thousands of Starbucks
across the globe in which latté suffering is creating harmful ripple effects at this very moment . . .

A huge part of practicing nonviolence is getting more
and more comfortable with the basic fact of discomfort. We
have to learn how to relax when things go wrong for us—
there's just no choice. Well, actually there are two other
options for dealing with discomfort:

[1] We can mindlessly throw the pain we feel onto
someone else, or

[2] We can (try) to ignore and suppress the discomfort.

But Option [1] is violence toward other people and
Option [2] is violence toward ourselves. Both options will
cause our enemies to multiply in the network of interdependence. An important purpose of the practice of nonviolence is to constantly debunk the myth that there's a way
to make it through life without ever having to feel pain or
discomfort.

Think about this. Let me know if you meet someone
who's never had anything go wrong for them. I don't believe
anybody has ever found a way to escape not getting what
they want, not even queens, movie stars, or billionaires. Even
Michael Jordan must've stubbed his toe on the way out of
the locker room once and gotten pissed off at the towel boy
for it. Somehow we all struggle with this basic truth that
pain and imperfection are part of this thing called life.

So we all get angry, and the moment of anger hurts

big-time. But if we act on the anger too quickly, what we're really doing is just handing the pain we feel off to someone else, like some sadistic quarterback. "Here, I want you to have this feeling; it sucks!" Acting impulsively on anger also results in us losing the only way we have to gain access to the natural wisdom of anger.

One of the most important things that meditation allows us to do is actually rest nonreactively with a moment of anger. This isn't fun to do, but it brings insight. It's sort of like being a zoologist: you're staying close to a dangerous but beautiful animal so that you can study it thoroughly. Resting with anger means that when we notice it boiling, we come back to the perceptions of the body. We breathe. Maybe we scream "!@#$%" in our mind, and then come back to placing our attention on the specific, concrete texture beneath our feet, our bodies in space, our breathing. We scream again, curse the gods, our congressman, and whoever else might spring to mind. Then we breathe again and feel our jaw-muscles loosening . . . then we rage once again, and breathe, and rest. We wait and wait until the eruption cools down. The reason we do this isn't because we're learning how to be doormats; it's because we know that if we don't rest our minds, there's very little chance of anything good coming out of it. Something bad will happen. That bad thing is called violence, and it comes with the animalistic impulse to ignore interdependence.

Resting, coming back to the sensations of the body, doesn't mean we never examine our anger. To use the fuel of anger's intelligence, we look at what's happened. Otherwise we'll be stuck with passive-aggressive behavior and pseudo-equanimity. But later, when we analyze, we have to examine each event individually, with our contemplative powers firmly rooted in an interdependent frame of reference—which means we look at the event from the perspective of those who disagree with us. We have to be willing to examine the other side of the coin: a complete picture never arises from a single point of view. What brought the *other* point of view into place? What made them act the way they acted?

A warning sign that we've fallen into one-sidedness is when we find ourselves saying to ourselves something like: "She *always* does this bullshit!" The truth is that nobody *always* does *anything*. Because of the fluid, ever-changing nature of interdependence, each event, each moment is like a new fractal pattern. Each interaction is constructed by a new and unique set of interwoven circumstances. You could waste a ton of your cell-phone minutes being righteous, complaining and ranting, and never once really looking at the other person's point of view. Using your minutes this way is very good for the phone company, but very bad for both you and the object of your rant.

We could try a little meditation session before attempting to analyze the situation that we're upset about. Even a few short minutes help. It's only in this more settled, interdependent examination that the wisdom of anger can be seen. For the intelligence of our anger to be utilized, a shift in motivation needs to occur. The wisdom of anger comes shining through only when the following condition is satisfied: we want to be *helpful* even more than we want to be *right*. Of course, this rule sucks too, because who doesn't want to be right? Everybody wants truth and justice on their side, but nobody said practicing nonviolence was easy. Ideally, we'd be both right *and* helpful, and also get a standing ovation for our efforts. Usually, when practicing nonviolence, we don't get to be both.

In my experience, the satisfaction of being right about what happened is fleeting, hollow, and irrelevant. We only crave that satisfaction because we don't think we can trust our own intelligence. We can trust that we have a clear perception without needing to tell everyone about it to make sure that we possess wisdom. Righteousness never acknowledges the full truth of what happens between individuals. When it comes down to it, the wisdom of anger is about wanting to be helpful, first and foremost. Being right is gravy. Being righteous is useless.

WHAT ABOUT dealing with other people's anger? The subway (or any form of mass transportation) is a good place to witness this. Someone knocks into you and then gets mad at you for being in the way. And then he glares at you, expecting reciprocal aggression back from you. Anytime someone pushes, he is expecting—on some level—to be pushed back. This is a basic principle of the way in which oppositional forces can reliably oppose one another. If there is no reactive force, there is no conflict.

As the recipient of violence, we're supposed to just deliver our line and get angry in return, playing our part in the melodrama. The high-noon showdown is set up, and right on cue, the other person has already drawn his pistol of rage, expecting you to whip out your own. But instead, you pull out a water gun. You don't offer the scripted oppositional force necessary for the moment of aggression to perpetuate itself into violence. There is nothing against which the initial aggression can push to further gain momentum.

Of course, this only works if the gun in question isn't a real gun, which, fortunately, it usually isn't. It also only works if we don't have anything to prove. With nothing to defend we offer a different type of space, and maybe humor, and the violence has no choice but to fizzle in that space. Maybe the aggressor even hears the hollow echo of his useless rage.

The way to practice receiving someone else's aggression is to find little ways to improvise, to not do what the action-movie script in your head calls for. On the subway the pushy person bumps into you and growls and you . . . smile and say good morning? You have nothing to lose (do you really care what a stranger on the subway thinks of you?), and you both have everything to gain through your practice.

ALTHOUGH the practice of interdependence is up to each of us on the level of self, we also have to continuously question the larger, systemic institutions and infrastructures that serve to perpetuate violence. These extend way beyond the inconvenience of getting bumped into on the subway. There is no surer sign of a society in decline than one that builds prisons faster than schools, as happens in many American states. In the face of these larger-scale global and societal problems, it might seem trite to talk about violence in terms of latté suffering or subway shenanigans. But we have to keep coming back to the connection between the big picture of society and the little picture of our own life and actions.

In the short term, one person can't do much about systems so deeply engrained in our cultural lexicon that they will probably take many generations to unravel, like the military/industrial complex. But if we want any chance of solving these problems in the long term, we have to use meditation to dismantle the scaffolding of the ego/aggression complex in our own minds.

CHAPTER 8:
GOTTA GET PAID

It is difficult to get a man to understand something when his salary depends upon his not understanding it.

UPTON SINCLAIR

MY COLLEGE FRIEND WAS ALWAYS SOCIALLY conscious, and not just the way most of us are with our occasional acts of community service. He felt that grinding urge—that sushi-roll mix of guilt and responsibility—to help other people, especially children. In college, while most people were partying, he was volunteering for kids at an urban community center. All his friends thought he would be the type of visionary person who someday would start his own organization dedicated to kids.

After college, my friend won a grant to spend a year outside of the United States. He spent the year working with homeless minors in Asia. He also became familiar with various NGOs (Non-Governmental Organizations) that worked with kids. The year had a huge impact on him.

When he got back home, my friend did something none of his old friends understood at first: he landed a job at a top investment banking firm. Strange choice, we thought, but he told us he felt he needed to learn more about how the corporate world worked—to gain skills, vocabulary, and connections that he would one day use in his work with children.

We figured that he knew what he was doing. But as the months went by, we watched him get more and more depressed. He was working so hard, and for something he didn't believe in at all. He told us that he thought his job was fake, the people he worked with uninspired. He wanted to quit. It probably didn't help that he was living again in his parents' apartment. Eventually, just to make it through the day, he would go into the bathroom in the morning, take his mother's lipstick from its case, and write "FUCK YOU" in bright burgundy letters on his bare chest. Then he would throw on his business-casual shirt, button it down and tuck it in, and head off to another long day at the office. Seriously.

After about six months at the job, he couldn't take it anymore. When he quit, he moved back to Asia, and began once again working with children. A year later he was back in New York City for a visit. Something had changed: he was definitely much happier than I'd seen him in a long time. It was the kind of happiness that comes from knowing the effort you put in on a daily basis is substantial, fulfilling, and real—there's a direct pipeline between your heart and your work. As we stood on a subway platform, trains rushing by and two homeless people stretched out asleep on the benches next to us, he told me about the challenges involved in working for the organizations in these communities. He described the grittiness of the communities he worked in and the chaos he often encountered. But his main obstacle was the bureaucracy within and funding of the organizations themselves. As we talked more, global interdependence became the glaring theme.

These NGOs relied on grants from large American foundations to do their work. These foundations received their money from large U.S. corporations—both through direct donations and indirectly through the wealth that corporations generated for individual donors to offer to the foundations. At this time, six months after 9/11, the U.S. economy was in a recession and the stock market was at a low point. This meant that corporate profits were low, that the foundations were receiving less money, and that the NGOs in Asia had less resources to work with. The irony of it all was that my friend's ability to do the work that he now loved, that fulfilled him, was dependent on the flourishing of corporations like the very investment firm he couldn't stand. What my friend loved doing with his life's energy depended *completely* on someone else doing work for which he had no respect. Ironic.

Together on a subway platform, he and I could only laugh. If you start paying attention to interdependence, it might make all your ideas collapse, and when that happens, laughter may be the only appropriate response.

WITH THE HEADLINE, "Marxist Student Has Capitalist Parents," the satirical newspaper *The Onion* brilliantly summarized the twenty-first-century dilemma of right livelihood. That kind of irony was something that often struck me about activism on university campuses. Those of us on the progressive end of the spectrum would go protest some company or business policy, but really could only be there in the first place because our parents could afford the exorbitant price of college tuition. For our parents to be able to do that, it was more than likely that they either worked for, held stocks in, or were in some other way supported by many of the companies that earned our disapproval. People on scholarships were supported by donors with the same sources of wealth. In other words, the companies we were protesting were ultimately sponsoring our protest.

The basic question of making a living is this: Do we apply our life's energy in a way that connects us with interdependence, or in a way that allows us the false comfort of hiding from it? When we start thinking about our life's energy, we have to discuss where we put the bulk of our waking hours. We have to talk about what we do for a living.

It's safe to say, most people I know don't like their jobs (except for the starving artists and a few others, who like their work but are frustrated that the world doesn't support it more). So many people feel alienated and disconnected from what they do with those 40 or 50+ hours each week. They feel little or no link between their inspiration for life and the actual products of their strenuous labor. On the other hand, the Buddhist understanding of exertion implies a consistently enthusiastic connection to what we do, like those seven dwarves singing happily on their way to the mines. This enthusiasm is what helps us to not cave in to resignation and apathy. This is the energy that makes our life's work meaningful and fulfilling to us, as well as beneficial to others.

When people start meditating and studying Buddhism, there's a tendency to feel even *more* disconnected from what we do for a living. When we start investigating interdependence—taking the idea of cause and effect seriously—we might become *slightly horrified* when we follow the effects of our labor on the world around us.

A friend of mine was the design director for a fashion magazine. When she became seriously interested in meditation and Buddhism, she felt a sharpened sense that what she did for a living was, in her own words: "Not good, for anyone, on any level." She felt she was getting paid (a lot) to manipulate people's perceptions, to make other women feel awful about themselves. What worried her the most was that she was becoming amazingly talented at it! She was pretty sure that she couldn't be an ethical Buddhist and keep that job.

When we take the time to investigate our livelihood, it might become apparent that our hard work supports certain (un)ethical structures that we wouldn't support in our personal lives. That can require a lot of guilt and denial to make it through each day. Maybe we feel it is impossible to use our work to make a positive difference. Within such hopelessness, we figure we can make enough money to support ourselves and loved ones. At the very least we can provide some immediate comfort for ourselves, if not something more deeply meaningful through our work. Or maybe we realize that even though we don't feel personally connected to the product of our effort, our work is providing livelihood and support for others, both nearby and far away. Or else we think we're slaving away for the devil incarnate and there's simply no way out of our capitalistic servitude. However, as my friend's realization about the NGOs demonstrates, the existence of that which we consider saintly labor is so deeply entwined with whatever we consider the devil's work that any attempt to segregate them eventually falls apart in laughter.

BUDDHIST ETHICS PLACE A HUGE EMPHASIS on engaging in a livelihood that can be morally reconciled with the following simple tenets:

[1] causing as little harm as possible and

[2] benefiting others.

Sounds easy enough. But it's always been difficult to determine which specific vocations were deemed "right" on this basis and which were "wrong," in that they caused more harm than good within the network of interdependence. The complexity of this issue has led to some famously strange ideas of right and wrong livelihood. Some Buddhists have "solved" the dilemma in truly ridiculous ways.

There is a widespread story that in Tibet it was considered harmful to be a butcher—a wrong livelihood—yet almost the entire population ate meat. Meat-eaters absolved themselves of the consequences of the death of the animal by their relative distance from the death. It was generally considered karmically "clean" if you were at least "three hands" removed, three intermediary people away from the death of the animal. Furthermore, people from the small Muslim population of Tibet were enlisted to perform the task of butchering, so that Buddhists wouldn't have to do it! This way of thinking led to a mistaken belief that there was somehow an independence—a distancing disconnect of cause and effect—between the act of killing an animal and the "end user" consuming the meat.

The questions here have nothing to do with whether eating meat is right or wrong. The two important questions here are:

[1] Are we aware of the connection between our consumption and how someone else must labor to produce what we consume?

[2] At the same time, do we see a connection between what our labor produces and what other people are able (or not able) to have?

The decision to slaughter is never made by the butcher; it's derived from a number on a spreadsheet in some corporate headquarters, predicting the demand for meat. The eater—not the butcher—has to be viewed as the primary cause of the animal's death; there's no way around this basic fact of market economics. And this is fine—as long as we consumers take responsibility for the death, and deeply acknowledge that there is blood on our hands, even if it's been sanitized by cellophane. This is perhaps the greatest lesson that interdependence has to offer us about right livelihood (and right living in general) in the twenty-first century: no person, and no profession, comes out completely clean, ever. On the other hand, no one is inherently defiled.

Of course, we as a culture often view certain professions as being inherently "cleaner" and "more meaningful" than others. There are some jobs in which it seems people get more automatic credit for engaging in right livelihood. If the compassionate activity is right in front of your face, then you, anointed by public perception, are making a worthwhile living. If you're an artist, you're at the very least pursuing your passion. If you're a nurse or you teach in a difficult public school, for example, you are credited with have a caring, important job. If you are the CEO of an oil company . . . not so much!

But where does this distinction come from, really? There are plenty of apathetic public school teachers and careless nurses. And so long as we who are dependent on the oil companies for fuel are in such a role, the provision of oil (or hopefully alternative energy) could conceivably manifest as a greatly compassionate activity, every bit as much as caring for the sick and dying. After all, how would the ambulance bring people to the hospital without fuel?

If our work provides something valuable to society, then our labor has a meaning. On the other hand, if we are doing *whatever we're doing* just for the money, the work will become meaningless sooner or later. The almighty dollar, after all, is just an abstracted valuation of our life's energy. We should never be living for an almighty abstraction.

The warped nature of modern labor is something that economic thinkers have talked about, at least since Marx and Engels. The alienation of labor occurs any time the inspiration for a person's labor is divorced from the actual product of that exertion. For example, a woman making sneakers in an Indonesian sweatshop might not be making sneakers because she wants to provide the joy of sports to the world. She might be doing it to make just enough money to avoid starving to death. Her motivation for her labor is therefore divorced from the product of her labor. In that separation, there is alienation, dissatisfaction, and suffering.

For most of us, the separation between the inspiration for our labor and the product of our labor probably isn't as extreme as the above example. But it might be apparent nonetheless. To investigate this, we have to consider the types of divisions we erect in our mind regarding the usage of our time and energy. When we look closely, we can see that our time is divided mentally into arbitrary distinctions of meaningless/meaningful or work/leisure. When the divides run deepest, then we consciously split our time each workweek into two categories: a) the disconnected tasks we do in our work life and b) the "meaningful" activities of our life—in which the money from work lets us participate—associated with loved ones, important causes, and personal interests. Very few of us say "I get to go to work now." Most of the time, labor is a matter of duty and toil.

This distinction of meaningful/meaningless time is one way we falsely segregate secular reality from sacred truth. In this way, we all have a little of Dr. Jekyll and Mr. Hyde in our work life. Sacred are all of the things that fulfill you in life—family, hobbies, wellness practices, spirituality, creative pursuits, and so on. Secular are all the things you do to provide the means for the sacred, i.e. the burden of your daily grind. Within this dichotomy, what you have to do is forever bland and mundane (and it always seems to take too much of your time), while what you feel fulfilled by doing is radiant and holy (and there's never enough time for it). The mundane labor provides the means for the existence of the holy (even if it's just a little time to yourself). In this state of mind, your labor is fundamentally, definitionally separated from a meaningful existence.

Whenever we mentally compartmentalize our work away from our more creative or more spiritual being, we construct a false dichotomy. This schism has to collapse on the level of universal interdependence. If your week and life are segregated this way, you're going to cause suffering—at the very least for yourself. You'll guiltily and resentfully acquiesce to your place in the world.

In such a state of mind, we're going to come to pro-foundly resent the time we spend working. Work will always be viewed as a means to a more meaningful life, rather than meaningful or beneficial in itself. And the nature of resentment is that it always eventually ferments into apa-thy and disillusionment. Apathy is a huge enemy to seeing interdependence. A Buddha finds deep meaning in her life not just during her free time or on vacation, but 168 hours each week. That's 10,080 minutes per week—for all the clockpunchers.

Where is all of this leading us in terms of getting paid and making a living? The lesson of interdependence on this issue comes down to a very simple—but very tricky—statement: "It's not what you do but how you do it." As consumers, if we support the existence of something in the world, then we rely on somebody to produce and deliver it to us. If you eat meat, then you can't avoid the fact that you *are* the butcher, even if you never see a bloody cleaver.

For myself and my friends who like to rant against oil companies, the problem is not the *existence of the companies*. The problem is how those companies make their decisions about ecology, and how much profit their shareholders think it is necessary to have, and how those decisions lead directly to wars and oppression. Somebody has to make decisions about what happens at these companies. And who makes them? *People* make them, based on certain value judg-ments, as well as predictions of what you and I (the mar-ket) will be willing to accept.

So the interdependent perspective on right livelihood is not "Quit your job and head for the nearest cave, and get some else to deliver you your daily meat." That's avoiding the whole issue of cause and effect! If we want to really make an impact on the world, then our perspective should be: "Practice mindfulness and awareness, and develop insight into love and compassion. And also, while you're at it, if you can, become the CEO of a company, and be the change you wish to see in how things are done."

Of course, given the way companies function, this change is only possible if the principles and interests guiding corporations shift from being centered on profit to being centered on the morality of interdependence, which means benefit (profit) to all the communities we and they share. And that movement relies on each company's stockholders beginning to deepen their practices of generosity to overcome the hungry-ghost mentality, because these stockholders happen to also be consumers. Thus consumers have to demand changes in the M.O. of the companies we collectively control. So, our practices of generosity and livelihood (in other words, consumption and production) are . . . well . . . *connected.*

WHAT MAKES THE STATEMENT "It's not what you do but how you do it" so complicated?

It seems the work environment of some professions is not inherently conducive to practicing interdependence or helping others. This must have been the initial intent behind Tibet's cultural agreement that butchering was not right livelihood. Over time, it must have become accepted that doing this work engrained violence in the mind of the person wielding the cleaver. But this fails to resolve the hypocrisy of meat-eaters not accepting personal responsibility for the existence of butchers.

That friend of mine who became disillusioned with her fashion-magazine job felt that her workplace necessarily fostered manipulation, jealousy, and skin-deep values in the people who worked there. She believed she wasn't "advanced" enough as a practitioner (whatever that might mean) to bring her practice into her work, without the benefits of her practice being nullified by the overbearing density of the existing culture.

Many young idealists who enter certain professions—like politics or business, for instance—say that they quickly discover that the requirements for ascending to a position of power requires much moral compromise. After enough compromise, one's initial positive intention gets assimilated into that profession's pre-existing order. The system can change us before we have any chance to change the system.

Some professions might seem pretty irreconcilable with the principle of interdependence. If you're considering becoming a pimp, or if you've ever read the book *Confessions of an Economic Hitman*, those might not seem like very beneficial lines of work to be in, no matter how you spin it.

But as for my friend at the fashion magazine, if she weren't doing her job, someone else would have it. No matter what we think the "better world" we'd like to see looks like, it will probably include magazines or some other form of communicative media like them (I hope). People will probably still wear clothing in this "more enlightened" society, so there will also probably be folks who care about fashion and want to have a forum for discussing it. If you believe in the effects of an individual's actions, then ask yourself a question: who would you rather have in these positions—someone who is trying to foster mindfulness and compassion in themselves and the world around them, or someone who hasn't (yet) connected to practicing those principles?

When we get overwhelmed by the larger moral implications of our work, we overlook the smaller, more imperceptible effects of our labor. Interdependence is about the little things you do. It's not just what you produce, but how you treat the people around you, who labor with you. And there is always something we can do that is positive—*ALWAYS*. We can't forget the radically empowering effects of recognizing interdependence, because the increase in awareness has the ability to bring new potential to even the tiniest grain-of-sand moments.

Running for the hills is not the way to go. We live in a time where there are actually fewer and fewer places left to run away to. Therefore, it's imperative to find ways to use your energy to dive into—not run from—existing paths of livelihood. A hip-hop mogul or an oil executive are powerful already. There's no reason they couldn't be powerfully selfless and compassionate as well.

CHAPTER 9:
CUTTING THROUGH INFOTAINMENT

I said: Where'd you get your information from, huh?

BEASTIE BOYS

OUR CONNECTION TO DIRECT KNOWLEDGE about the world we live in is superficial, to say the least. Most of us have very little idea of exactly what is going on in our own community, much less around the globe. We often lack the necessary knowledge to put world events into any larger context. The news treats emerging conflicts as if they were volcanoes spewing forth spontaneously, rivers of lava coming up from nowhere. It is very rare to find news coverage that places new events in the framework of an interdependent historical narrative. And increasingly, our sense of content regarding the world around us comes not from seeing, feeling, and touching, but from Googling and YouTubing.

Can we fully believe what we read scrolling across a headline news ticker? Can a four-word headline ever convey a truly interdependent picture of reality? And did you ever wonder why you need to be told what's going on in a war-zone by someone who has to spend an hour in hair and makeup before she can tell you? Why can't we see the thousands of dead bodies that war produces? Does information really require sanitization and plastic wrapping in order to be digestible by the public?

If we are truly curious about cause and effect, our practice of awareness must include an investigation into how we come to gain certainty in whatever we profess to know for sure. Sometimes, when we start to investigate, we have to admit that we don't really know much of anything, even though we usually formulate a view of world events on the basic premise that we "know" a lot.

Infotainment is a dangerous and powerful word. It points to a phenomenon that Buddhism has been investigating since long before the Internet and television were around, centuries before the term came into being. At its heart, infotainment represents the indiscriminate combination of two mental longings, conflated by our ignorance. These two impulses are:

[1] the impulse to be informed—to know what is real and what isn't, in ourselves and the world around us (the "info"); and

[2] the desire to be entertained and comforted, to be reassured about the correctness of our personal and collective tendencies (the "tainment").

We've already looked at entertainment on a more superficial level as an escape-based enemy to discipline. Here we're examining the challenge of entertainment on a much deeper level of habit. As far as truth and wisdom are concerned, entertainment is a ploy to maintain an inner status quo of the mind, to absorb only the information that confirms our various positions, and to ignore or edit out that which challenges our perspective. On this deeper level, entertainment points to a need for comfort and certainty in our pre-existing view of the world. Entertainment is about the coziness of seeing only what we want to see, knowing only what we wish to know.

There is a tremendous danger in enmeshing the quests for information and entertainment in our minds. There is great tension inherent between these two forces. The desire to be informed is about knowing what is true, plain and simple. Wisdom is about seeking truth whether or not the seeker himself is vindicated or comforted by the unveiling of that truth. This desire to know—even if some knowledge is highly uncomfortable—is what makes the quest for wisdom so courageous and challenging.

On the other hand, the desire to be entertained is all about feeling good about our assumptions. It's about sugar coating the mind that is being entertained. Entertainment never requires a reality check. By definition, entertainment can't ever provoke any real challenges to the individual who is being entertained. A challenge to our assumptions is just that: *challenging*.

Sometimes what the truth of interdependence reveals to us is just uncomfortable about the life we're living and the society we are participating in—no *ifs*, *ands*, or *buts*. It constantly calls my own foolish actions into question. So there is a deep friction between information and entertainment. Real information only comes when I'm willing to have the quest for knowledge actually bump up against my own identity and beliefs. Real information only comes if I'm willing to find what exists beyond my comfort zone. Real information doesn't always make me feel so great about myself or my place in the world.

Infotainment is what happens when our mind receives information and then only takes truth of the type and in the forms that it finds palatable. Reality gets coated in syrup to make it go down more easily. One of the most interesting things about the mind that succumbs to infotainment is that its biases and modes of filtering direct experience can be incredibly subtle. Biases inhabit a blind spot that can only be revealed by a systematic broadening of self-awareness. And self-awareness can only reveal those blind spots if we truly allow our assumptions to be challenged. We all have our own ways of making truth fit into soundbites, and personal slogans. In this way, thoughts are our private news headlines.

As we begin to notice through meditation, our conscious perception is manufactured and packaged by our habitual biases. These filters make it very difficult to see things from any other perspective, because we aren't even aware that we began our investigation with a framed bias. We could think all along that our connection to the facts of the matter is completely direct and objective, and the whole time we're filtering reality through our preferred way of thinking. We do this not because it is necessarily beneficial, even for us, but because it is familiar. That which is familiar grants a tense pseudo-comfort. When these mental biases become collectivized through channels of mass media, the worldview of an entire society can be sugar coated by infotainment. In this case, a path for increasing self-awareness—for wanting to challenge ourselves—is the only way to avoid an Orwellian outcome.

Thinkers like Noam Chomsky have argued for many years that there are many structural filters built into the systems of journalism both in the United States and elsewhere. As we have seen, the perverse beauty of a habitual filter—whether mental or systemic—is that it can be invisible. Filters are not only invisible to the one receiving the information; they are invisible as well to the one *presenting* the information. As Chomsky notes, the result is that individual news reporters can honestly believe that they are reporting events straightforwardly, with no bias at all. Reporters can do this because all of the systemic biases of their sources and methods of dissemination are invisible to them in daily activity. Thus, they can uphold the norm of the system's biases, without any awareness that they are doing so.

The same thing is true of the filters that govern the way the human mind functions when self-awareness is underdeveloped. An untrained mind is just *waiting* to be spun. Our inner Fox News shows us what we expect and want to see and just tells us what we were certain we already knew. Meanwhile, another person's inner NPR conveys a different story. Our minds have been colonized for so long that we wave only the colored flags of familiar thoughts and deem any perspective that doesn't fit with our assumptions to be deeply "unpatriotic."

CONSIDER THIS classic thought experiment: We walk into a darkened room and think we see a poisonous snake slithering along the floor. Immediately we launch into a

fearful fury over the snake, and carry out all of our subse-
quent actions on the premise that the snake is plotting to
kill us. We arm ourselves, rave like lunatics, and get ready to
start a WAR ON SNAKES (picture the Fox News coverage).
Then someone comes along and remembers to turn on a
light in the room. The fearsome snake turns out to be a
gnarled rope someone left lying around.

This image for infotainment is made all the more sinister by contemporary media. Within our twenty-first century
modes of communication, truth can be easily manipulated
and framed to get the viewer of the information to receive
it in a predetermined way, to elicit a desired spin of "truth."
Turning on the light doesn't guarantee the clarifying of confusion anymore. If all of the media of our societal experience make us believe that a rope is a snake, then a rope
becomes a snake, either in darkness or the light of day.

The question is, how do we turn on that metaphorical
light in the room for ourselves and others in an age where
meanings, phrases, and symbols can be so easily rearranged,
so perfectly edited and explosively delivered for maximum
effect? Seeing our own biases stops the spin.

IN SANSKRIT, the word *prajna* describes the kind of
intelligence that can see through all the carefully edited
information that's constantly coming at us. *Prajna* literally
means "best knowing." We are equipped with a mental sen-
sor capable of separating the wheat of direct experience
from the chaff of confused ideas with little to no basis in
reality. Prajna intuitively sees the difference between genuine intention and subtle perversions. This is a capacity that
arises out of self-awareness to cut through all façades to the
essence of an experience or event.

This wisdom of discernment doesn't just come from knowing what's going on in the big picture of societal media. It comes into play in the really simple choices we make all the time. Can you tell a van Gogh painting from a Basquiat? When is it the right time to tell a joke or to keep my mouth shut? How do we read people's faces to see if they're in a bad mood? All of these simple observations require a type of discernment that only comes from direct experience of the phenomena at hand. We have to be able to intuit the important features in each situation, and have a method for actually distinguishing mistaken ideas from direct experience.

We also have to be able to have awareness of the larger context in which our judgments arise. In the case of my love of good falafel, I have to begin to look into my own falafel-prejudice. I might not make a choice to determine the quality of a falafel sandwich based on how tasty or filling the falafel actually is. Instead, I might make my choice based on the physical attractiveness of the person serving me. That's falafel infotainment. With no awareness of the context in which fine distinctions arise, we can be so easily manipulated and only allow ourselves to see or feel what we wanted to see (or, worse still, what someone else wants us to see).

The judgments and choices we make are still fully subjective and personal. My definition of a good falafel sandwich arises from my sense of what the most crucial features of falafel are, which might be very different from your idea of a good falafel sandwich. You might not even like falafel at all,* which could be every bit a mark of your intelligence as demand for a good tahini sauce is a mark of mine.

* ARE YOU CRAZY?

There is a kind of wisdom called Ultimate or Transcendent Prajna. This refers to a state of observation and communication in which the subject completely and steadily realizes his/her own subjectivity within the network of interdependent perspectives. As we ourselves see truth, we also see *through* ourselves. Our own subjectivity becomes transparent; we become able to *both see our bias and see through our bias* (this is very different from the confused state of merely *believing* we see through it). Within this way of perceiving information, all of our points of view are fluid and nondogmatic, ready to change when the network of reality presents a new and unscripted moment. This ultimate wisdom sees the highest level of interdependence. Somebody who lives full-time in this state of wisdom simply cannot be manipulated, cannot be bought, cannot be sold ideas. This kind of person has nothing left to defend—except compassion. In this state, we are no longer begging to be comforted by the information we take from experience. We are immune to the expensively staged, aircraft-carrier photo-ops of infotainment, because we are constantly relinquishing our need to end up on the pretty side of truth.

When Siddhartha Gautama was interviewed by pundits about how he could trust the deep truths that he purported to *know for sure*, he reached down silently and gently touched the ground, as if to say that the Earth was the only source he needed. He could do this because he fully trusted his direct experience. It was a silent demonstration of a true and faultless "no spin zone." That's the kind of confidence in knowing that doesn't come from seeing something on a screen. It only comes from first-hand experience of the world. It can only happen when your words and your actions are in union. Otherwise, it's just an arrogant gesture.

There are always ways to become more aware of our own subjectivity—and it is is crucial we do so. One way to do this is to diligently search for multiple perspectives on any event or phenomenon before passing judgment. This will at least ensure that we have a diversity of subjective points of view to intelligently inform our belief. To do this diligent search, we have to actually *want* to know the truth, and be willing to put in the work it takes to discover it. If we're going to live a life in touch with interdependence, we are going to need to care very deeply about what is true and false, and where we get our information.

We have to develop confidence that we can trust our own moment-by-moment understanding of the world we live in. Otherwise, the information we use as beacons in the navigation of life will constantly lead us in the wrong direction, leaving us hopelessly confused about the difference between truth and ignorance. The only reason we care about overcoming our ignorance is because ignorance *just ain't bliss*. Ignorance leads us to a fundamental misalignment with reality. Ignorance will always cause suffering eventually. On the societal level, as the strands that weave together our globe become more and more finely entwined, the time-lag between our ignorant beliefs and the reverberations of suffering caused by them will keep becoming less and less. Ignorance's "don't ask, don't tell" policy might work for a little while, it won't serve us for very long.

We might ignorantly not care that oil and water are different types of liquid, until the house starts burning down. And in this house that we all share, the roof is most definitely on fire.

PERSONALLY, when I really start to get curious about things, I realize that I usually don't know as much for sure as I think I do. And the main thing I realize is that I don't even really know myself all that well. I'm not as aware as I would like to be of all the ways in which my own mind has been colonized. I can't yet touch the ground as my witness when it comes to full certainty in who or what I am. But awareness of uncertainty is itself an insight. Uncertainty is a sign of being in touch with the ever-changing nature of interdependence. Too bad some of our political leaders mistakenly find strength in claiming they know what is true for certain. This willingness to admit that we don't know something is why so many Buddhist teachers have likened wisdom to a childlike innocence or a "beginner's mind."

If we want to *actually* learn something new, the first step is to humbly accept that we may not *know* what we claim to be sure about. We have to really want to see the ways that our understanding of the world has been colonized. Then, we have to actually see that there might be perspectives we haven't considered, and explore those. The best way to do this formally is through a series of meditation techniques known collectively as contemplative meditation, where we specifically give ourselves the space and precision to examine our own beliefs and reactions around certain key issues.

There are many techniques of contemplation, and doing them on a consistent basis has the awareness-expanding effect of heightening the contrast between what we *know* and what we think we "know." Then we can begin to take those techniques out into the collective media that we use to communicate with one another, to offer critiques of the profit-oriented delivery of information in our society. Practicing meditation can be a way to call out inaccuracies, perversions, and biased edits in ourselves and the world we share. We do this by constantly taking it upon ourselves to collect multiple perspectives of information and events—personal, interpersonal, communal, and global. And we especially commit to staying in touch with those sources of information that are uncomfortable or problematic.

WE DON'T HAVE THE LUXURY of examining and analyzing the sources of our information forever. Life is constantly calling us to act, to make decisions based on the best information we can find about what's going on around us. What we do must spring from our ideas and experiences about what is real, what is good and bad, what we can trust and what we can't. We have to learn to trust ourselves, and find ways to trust the compassionate intelligence of those around us.

Interdependence will constantly surprise you, and it will rarely vindicate your long-held positions and beliefs. Want to practice living in a fluid network? Then be willing to *not know*. Even when we do know something based on direct experience at this moment, we don't know it forever. To reframe something Stephen Colbert said, if our intelligence tells us that something is true on Monday, and we receive new information on Tuesday, then the belief we hold on Wednesday should be flexible enough to accommodate this shift in causes and conditions. Otherwise, our intelligence will ossify into dogma, and the only "news" we'll be willing to get will be the "news" we always wanted to hear. Truth will be censored and manipulated until we're hopelessly out of touch with reality. This is a most unfair and unbalanced way to live.

CHAPTER 10:
FEARLESSNESS IS NOT BROUGHT TO YOU BY REEBOK

Please understand, I never had a secret chart
to get me to the heart of this or any other matter.

LEONARD COHEN

WHEN I WAS EIGHT YEARS OLD, I memorized the Major League Baseball rulebook. For about a month I was convinced that my destiny lay in becoming a professional baseball umpire. I got a thrill out of the confidence that came from knowing the intricacies of the rules, all the definitive ifs, ors, and buts from which the detailed structure of the game was crafted. Baseball's playing field was well defined and dependable, and while the iterations of what could happen were immense, the rules dictate the objective truth, the meaning of each event, based on a set of clearly defined regulations. Is he safe, or is he out? There aren't any other possibilities, always exactly one right call for the umpire to make. One winner, one loser, nothing else can result.

Being an umpire is basically robotic. You don't interpret ambiguous scripture; you see things clearly, objectively, and proclaim a firm decision. Within that mechanical mode of judgment, there is something almost divine. The clarity of the rules allows the umpire the power to believe that there is always a prescribed answer in any situation: just read what the rulebook says.

Eventually my own sense of reality as a playing field with strictly defined rules started to erode. Maybe it happened the first time I had an unrequited crush on a girl, or the first time I tried to write a real poem. It may've been when I realized that my parents were not, in fact, omniscient giants. They were just fumbling through life as best they could, and had no hallowed rulebook to guide them. When I started meditating, my belief that I could forever master the rulebook fell away for good.

The overarching implication of the truth of interdependence is that reality is never static. The structure of the reality rulebook is constantly shifting. There is no fixed moral hook to hang our hat upon. The idea that right and wrong are relative phenomena could lead us into a deep and inescapable apathy. The apparent emptiness of this realization could turn us all into hedonists in a hurry. Maybe we should just become like the Roman Empire before the fall, collapsing into a cartoonish orgy for as long as we can, until either death or the "barbarian" hordes overwhelm us.

But looking more deeply, the fact that everything is interdependent breeds a much greater sense of responsibility to get familiar with the way our own mind works, to use our individual and collective creative energies to find ways to connect instead of to isolate, to heal instead of harm. The playing field is ours, so what qualities do we want the game to reflect? Greed or compassion? Well-being or disease? Peace or war?

PRACTICING INTERDEPENDENCE is an ongoing process of getting and staying connected to the real Internet, getting connected to both ourselves and those around us. We have to practice it, not just think about it, because our habitual tendency to disconnect from ourselves and others—both personally and culturally—has enormous momentum. The process of connecting with the various levels of interdependence isn't an easy journey. It requires always moving toward choices, beings, and situations that are unfamiliar, always taking one more step beyond the walls of our comfort zone.

Practicing interdependence involves a lot of stepping into neighborhoods that we've never been in before (speaking both metaphorically and literally). It requires entering into situations we don't know much about to begin with, beyond our ideas of what might lie there. Practicing interdependence means constantly relinquishing our home-court advantage, departing from the familiarity of our usual ways of handling ourselves. And when we step into unknown neighborhoods, it's always going to make us feel off-balance, awkward, and uncomfortable. There's no way the unknown could do anything but make us feel awkward. And when uncertainty comes, we're definitely going to experience fear—as a whisper or a scream—each and every time a new experience comes into our mind, each time a new event blossoms in this vast network called reality. And in these moments, fumbling for the rulebook won't quell the fear.

Reebok used to have an advertising campaign that used the slogan "No Fear." (There's now a clothing company with the same name.) Other advertising campaigns have often linked their products or services to the conquest of fear. It's interesting to think that something like fearlessness has anything to do with what phone company you choose or a sitcom on UPN, but both have used the slogan "be fearless" in their print ads. It sounds good. The idea is that you could dive into any situation, like a heroic deep-sea diver, a brand-named Buddha, and always be victorious. With the old Reebok ads, it was as if the electricity would rise up from your cushion-aired hightops, enter your heart chakra, and rise up your spinal cord to your brain. All trembles and trepidation would be left behind in the dust. $120 for the requisite pair of sneakers that wore out after only three or four months was a small price to pay for the promise of never having to face fear again.

Fear is not to be dismissed. A moment of fear is actually a message that we are in a new and unfamiliar place within the network of interdependence. Fear is the awkwardness of stepping into a new neighborhood of our mind. Dismissing it actually keeps us comfortable for even less time than a poorly made pair of expensive sneakers. But if we let it in, something new and unexpected is bound to happen.

We've all had those amazing moments in which life becomes actual instead of theoretical. Our fantasies or nightmares about what was supposed to happen crumble in the face of what is actually happening. What might be or what should be gets KO'd by what is. These moments are collectively known as the present moment. When there's a difference between the theory of what was expected and the actuality of what is, we can be certain that a moment of fear will necessarily arise in the mind. Fear is the nature of new experiences. Even if it's just a tiny flicker of awkwardness, there will always be fear, every moment, as long as there are beings who live in a network of change and interdependence. To be a *being* inherently implies change and interdependence; these are the true brands of our existence. Getting connected necessarily means experiencing fear.

Real fearlessness is very different from what's being sold in the Reebok slogan. Real fearlessness is about how we respond to the inevitable arising of fear, instead of some misbegotten attempt to eliminate it. Fear becomes the inspiration to see that there is always more to be learned from living. Fear is the fuel for questioning ourselves, our actions, and our concepts about ourselves and others more and more deeply.

Of course, fear becomes none of these things if we try to hide from it, justify our way around it, or buy our way out of it. If we don't investigate our own life and place in the world we get buried alive in a coffin of unexamined fear. When we stay with the arising of fear long enough for it to connect us to something new, something unexpected or unfamiliar, something that makes us question long-held beliefs about who we are and what this world is, then we're in an undiscovered, yet-uncolonized realm. And when those moments come, the only thing that will matter is how much we have trained to open our heart and mind.

A DEFINITIVE HANDBOOK, describing exactly what activities to engage in for practicing interdependence, would be out of date the moment it was released. This book isn't that. Rather, this book is an invitation to start exploring how we can get more and more connected to seeing the truth of interdependence manifesting at all levels of our life, an invitation to explore living in accordance with those truths. We each must examine for ourselves our connection to each other, instead of blindly accepting theories or prescriptions that aren't based on our direct experience. In fact, the historical Buddha *demanded* that his students do this. If they wanted to call themselves his students, he insisted that they must never take his word for a single thing. Faith is no replacement for experience. If we want to know if it's raining outside, logging on to Weather.com is never going to be as good as just looking out the window.

Develop your own insights and live them in your own life. At the same time, we each have to practice interdependence with vigor and passion if we want to survive and thrive. As Dr. King said, interdependence is how our universe is structured. Any society that ignores the structure of the universe will come crashing down.

Mindfulness, awareness, insight, generosity, discipline, nonviolence, exertion, wisdom, and fearlessness are all essential and timeless qualities that transcend all contextual boundaries of our specific lifestyle. We need an ongoing systematic training to develop these qualities—they're not going to grow on their own out of nowhere.

The number one way to do this is to develop a daily practice of formal meditation. Try to find a meditation group near you with a teacher, atmosphere, and group energy to which you connect. There are groups like this in most North American cities. This will offer the support of *sangha*, a community of people to share experiences with as you explore interdependence and wisdom. It will also offer the support of an ongoing relationship with teachers who have some experience with Buddhism's vast body of knowledge. If you can't find a group near you, there are lots of other multimedia resources, books, podcasts, online teachings, and more. Ultimately, though, our practice should provide a way to connect with others, and a real live community is irreplaceable.

It's also crucial to make a time commitment to a ten-to-twenty minute meditation practice every day (yes, *every* day—or as close to it as possible). The benefits of doing this are slow and subtle, but the impact over time is profound. Try it. Try meditating for ten minutes each of the next fourteen days, and then don't meditate for a couple of days, and see how those days feel.

You might not think it's doing much of anything for you, until someone who knows you well says to you, "You know, you're much less of an asshole than you used to be."

EPILOGUE:
COUNTER-CULTURE VS.
TRANSFORMATIVE CULTURE

SOMETIMES I SEE MY OWN (BROADLY DEFINED) generation through two remarkably different lenses. When I feel a little cranky and depressed and I haven't gotten a good night's sleep in a while, it seems like we're all just going through the motions, endlessly surfing and browsing only to find the same old page all over again, twiddling our thumbs, tracing random doodles on mental sketchpads, dressing up and striking wasted poses that someone else has struck a thousand times before, just to somehow feel momentarily original within the hopeless unoriginality we've inherited. Sometimes it feels like we're subconsciously awaiting the arrival of an apocalypse that for some reason just won't get here and let us off the hook.

Then I take a nap, blink, breathe, and look again, and I see nothing but incredibly talented and creative people who are each fumbling in their own brilliance for ways to think, speak, and live from a deep and unyielding intention to exist meaningfully and compassionately for ourselves and others. We just aren't always on the same page about how to accomplish this.

The truth is probably somewhere in the middle of these two extremes, but like everything else that arises in the network of interdependence, it all depends on your perspective. Because I'm a reluctant optimist, and because my Buddhist teachers have hammered it into my head, I lean toward the latter way of looking as much as I can. If the world really is ultimately a co-production of the mind-states of all those individuals inhabiting it, then there is always hope for us, as long as each individual begins to feel the need to train his or her own mind. If we keep developing communities that organize around this principle (and if you can't find any, keep looking, they're there)—each individual taking the time to care for her own mind and then taking the time to care about the impact on others of her actions—things might start getting a lot brighter in a hurry.

We don't have the luxury of creating a counterculture anymore. The wish to erect a utopian counterculture that stands in opposition to a hated mainstream society falls apart on the ultimate level of interdependence; after all, these two cultures would depend on each other for their oppositional identities. Whatever language, symbolism, style of dress, and multimedia we could use to define ourselves as authentically "alternative" would be branded and sold back to us at retail before we even got our act together. It's happened so many times already. There is no way to counter the mainstream. Even the word *alternative* means "mainstream" now. This only leaves us with one choiceless choice: instead of *countering* the culture, we have to *transform* it. We have to use existing cultural forms to peel back the layers of the blazing digital façades and reveal the beating heart underneath.

There's nothing inherently wrong with a façade. The only problem with a façade arises when there's nothing but self-deception lying underneath. If our cultural symbols point to the heart of the matter, then they can transform self-absorption into the substance of real compassion every day of the week. To steal a line from the poet Saul Williams, in an age where everyone is trying to be hardcore—hardcore progressive, hardcore conservative, hardcore bungee jumper, hardcore punk, hardcore rap, hardcore vegetarian, hardcore Zen—we can consistently train in being "heartcore." Learning the shapeless difference between self-deception and authentic presence is the real work of fearlessness. If we master that process, our lives will become blazing four-dimensional billboards for the truth of interdependence, the embodiment of heartcore.

The Indian writer and activist Arundhati Roy said something in response to the slogan of many progressive movements, the oft-used "Another world is possible." She said: "Another world is not only possible, she is on her way. On a quiet day, I can hear her breathing." The universal truth of interdependence might add one more layer to this sentiment: Another world is definitely possible; it looks just like this one.

APPENDIX I:
GETTING STARTED WITH MEDITATION

PREPARING TO MEDITATE

FIND A GOOD, RELATIVELY QUIET, relatively neat place. A timer with a bell, beep, or flashing light is good so you don't even have to worry about looking at a clock. Commit to a length of time beforehand for this session and don't alter it unless there's a real emergency. If you want to do five minutes, that's wonderful, but commit to a length at the beginning and stick to it. Shrines (totally optional) are nice reminders of entering the space of meditation, but they have to be made personal—maybe a picture of someone who inspires you personally (Dr. King, your favorite aunt, your creative mentor—whatever you connect to) and reminds you of what is possible when a human being is able to really open her/his heart and mind. But keep the space simple. Buying lots of stuff from your local Tibetan store will not make you a better meditator. Only a personal relationship to the practice can do that.

BODY CHECK IN: Stand relaxed in front of your cushion with palms facing forward, accommodating the space in front of you. Let the knees microbend so that you can really feel the ground connecting to your feet. Scan upward from the soles of your feet to the crown of the skull. If there is a particular place of tension in the body, let your attention rest there a little longer and see what happens to the feeling when your attention is fully placed on it. After the scan, sit down (for a ten-minute session, this check-in can take just fifteen seconds).

MIND CHECK IN: Ask yourself "How am I?" and see what comes up. Remember that the question is not "How should I be?" If nothing comes up, fine. Just rest your attention in the space of the question. If something strong comes up, try to rest with the visceral feeling of it, rather than the narrative components of what a crazy boss you have or how your boyfriend is driving you nuts. This is a great practice to do on its own when we don't have time for a full session. (For a ten-minute session, this check-in can take just fifteen seconds; for a longer session, you can spend more time here, up to five minutes).

MEDITATION POSTURE

THE SEAT: The main thing about posture is a comfortable seat. Sit up high enough on a blanket, yoga blocks, pillows, or meditation cushion so that your sitz bones can really plug down into your seat without compromising the spine. Sit up high enough on cushions so that the knees are lower than the hip joints, and the legs can just get out of the way of the pelvis. Sit up a little higher than you usually do in sukhasana in yoga class, because you'll be here longer (make it easy . . . no points awarded for full lotus!). Make sure your ankles are padded by a blanket or mat (and the knees too if the knees are on the floor), which will ease the tendency of the feet to fall asleep. If you're in a chair, let the feet rest flat on the floor, hip-distance apart.

THE UPPER BODY: The spine lifts up out of the pelvis without breaking at the waist. Find the energetic balance where you are not slumping but not using every muscle in your upper body to hold yourself up. The chest is open but not puffed. The shoulder blades are dropping down the back but not pinching the spine. The skull is balanced on the atlas of the spine. The chin is just slightly contained inward without losing the balance of the skull or closing off the throat. Let your upper arms fall from the shoulders. Fold at the elbow and drop your palms lightly wherever they fall on the thighs. The face is relaxed; the lips are not pursed. The eyes release and the gaze softens and lowers to a little area on the floor about four feet in front of you. Our eyes accommodate what's in front of them without needing to chase what they see. If it is more comfortable, close your eyes—but if you do be very careful not to drift into fantasy or sleepiness.

WORKING WITH THE BREATH

Begin to place your attention on the breath. This isn't a pranayama breath exercise, but if you want to take some deep breaths to orient yourself, that's fine. Also, if you would like to focus your attention on the breath in a specific location in your body like the belly or nostrils, that may help you settle in as well. Or you can count breaths if you feel very scattered and distracted. However, if and when you feel a little more settled in the practice, try to place attention on the full cycle of each natural breath as it moves in the body, then let it go and place your attention on the next breath. Each breath is a thread, an anchor we can rely on to connect with the present moment. The breath is the definition of NOW, and we connect by feeling it, literally and physically.

WORKING WITH THINKING

[A] Thinking is not a problem.

[B] The moments when we notice our attention has left the breath are powerful successes, not failures. Our awareness is flexing its muscles.

[C] When these moments of awareness arise, acknowledge them by labeling, saying "thinking." Try to let the voice that says thinking be gentle and direct. Then, with mindfulness, gently guide the attention back to the simple act of breathing, placing the attention on the breathing body.

[D] If you find yourself saying "thinking" every two seconds like a nervous tic, relax the labeling technique and just come back to the flow of the breath whenever you realize that your mind has wandered. We are most concerned about the thoughts that really take us away from the breath, the moments we really go astray from the present. Those are the ones we need to acknowledge and guide ourselves back from.

[E] If the technique becomes too claustrophobia-inducing, let it go and come back to placing your attention on your body. Just be with yourself. Smile, if you have to. Then when you feel a little more relaxed, work again with the breath and the acknowledging and labeling of wandering into thoughts and fantasies.

APPENDIX II:
POST-MEDITATION PRACTICE OF INTERDEPENDENCE

POST MEDITATION— THE ATTITUDE OF CONFIDENCE

Arise from the session with some hint of trust that the practice of working with our mind this way is healthy and helpful. You don't need a lot of this trust, but if you don't have any of it, there isn't really any reason to do this practice. What good would it be?

CONGRATULATE YOURSELF for having been able to stay with a session for the predetermined amount of time. Try to find some way to connect with the attitude that the situations, trials, and tribulations of our life can all be dealt with sanely, with the same sense of presence, and the same willingness to engage in the ups and downs as they smack us in the face. Maybe, maybe there could even be a glimmer that everything we encounter in life can be a valid experience worthy of respect. Every experience is precious because our experience is what we *actually* have. This is the true mind of meditation (which will not always be calm and peaceful). This is what the great meditators of the past were able to open up to (slowly but surely). This is where they were able to abide. They call it the lion's roar of confidence.

THANKFULLY, we don't live our life on the meditation cushion, and for approximately twenty-three hours and forty-five minutes a day (when you're not doing a more intensive meditation "retreat"), the practice of interdependence occurs up off our asses. That is, after all, where the real fun begins.

While we can only discuss general principles as guidelines, the *actual* practice of interdependence involves making very specific choices throughout the day. It is inherently a practice of being political—not only in the conventional use of the word (although it certainly includes participation in the political process). Practicing interdependence requires constantly examining our lifestyle and making some decisions about what habits to cultivate and what to avoid.

Any time we make a decision with interdependence in mind, we are living a political choice. Voting for someone to represent us is merely an indirect (and often skewed and perverted) extension of the political choices implied by our way of living day in and day out. This type of interdependent politics is far more direct than voting for representatives once every few years. It even transcends the idea of voting with our feet or voting with our dollars. Moment by moment, we are each voting with our minds, casting ballots for the way we would like our community to manifest. This thing called Earth is just the democratic tally of the results of billions of mental votes. Of course, it's interesting in democratic societies how some people's votes seem to count much more than others. But awareness consistently empowers individuals to put our moment-by-moment mental votes to work in many more ways than we ever thought possible just by stepping into a voting booth.

When we begin to tackle the interdependent issues that matter to us, we need to be settled enough in our own minds and open enough in our intention that we don't only look at the problem from the colonization of our own biases, through the hazy filter of habit.

To take just one example, should people drive SUVs? From interdependence's viewpoint, the answer is a clear no. SUVs guzzle energy at a ridiculous rate (the statistics are unbelievable), pollute the environment and don't seem to really benefit anyone. Speaking personally, they are a behemoth symbol of the confused American myth of rugged INdependence. But some people I consider my friends happen to drive SUVs, so I can't just rave like a lunatic if I want to keep those friends (and I do want to keep them). And I'm not going to slash any tires to overthrow the tyranny of Chevy Suburbans (see the chapter on nonviolence). But I might have some real conversations with my SUV-driving friends in which we actually try to question the lives we are leading in a mutually supportive way. I should probably be up for examining my own beliefs and actions in these conversations as well. I should be curious enough to let some of my own bullshit be shouted out, too. I might actually even try to make some *new* SUV-driving friends and see where they're coming from and why they've made the choices they've made.

Maybe somebody's mind or ears are closed right now to new possibilities, which can be frustrating. Maybe we think we're surrounded by people who don't even seem aware that they *have* a mind—much less that they could actually open it. But that's no reason to stop practicing to open *our* own minds and keep the conversations going. What other options do we have?

In addition to engaging in societal issues and dialogues that spark me, I've found it very helpful to develop a personal set of small post-meditation practices to build awareness of the myriad links in the chains of cause and effect. These post-meditation practices challenge me to bring the principles of mindfulness and awareness into those other twenty-three hours forty-five minutes per day. They each take very little time, yet they can serve as ways to slow our mind down out of the roadrunner pace of movement and place our attention in the present moment, snapping us back into our connectedness like an elastic band. They also cause us to practice generosity by offering our ongoing presence. Never underestimate the power of your presence to shift the momentum of the minds of those around you. You should also never expect that your simple actions will enlighten anyone or save the world. So your practice should remain just that: a *practice*, a process, an experiment in being unbrandedly fearless.

HERE ARE THE THREE post-meditation practices that I try to remember every day.

[1] I try to question one consumption choice that I make every day. If I can refrain from consuming the chosen item, then I try to offer the money to a person or cause who needs it. If I don't refrain, I at least try to find a way to consume it that causes less suffering and more benefit in the network of interdependence. For instance, take one item of food you eat each day and see if it can be found locally and organically. This daily mindful consumption practice has led to a much greater curiosity about the structures of my consumption choices, as well as greater curiosity into the ethics of companies that I support financially.

[2] I pick up and dispose of three pieces of garbage that I did not create each time I go outside. Of course, this doesn't make NYC much cleaner. But it does cause me to slow down for a moment, to become aware of my concrete surroundings, and to apply mindfulness to a specific task. Most importantly, it gives me the opportunity to engage with the awkward emotions that arise in my mind from having to bend over and pick up a candy wrapper in front of others on a crowded street. This practice adds about four seconds to my commute.

[3] I try to say "thank you" every time a service is performed for me, every time I am part of a financial transaction. This cuts through any sense of entitlement, that money means I somehow own the people who serve me, reminding me that money is solely an abstraction of shared human energy that allows our interdependent needs to be met.

Three is a good number of practices. They should be short and simple, requiring the application of mindfulness in the present moment and awareness of your mind's role in your environment. Come up with your own list of three simple daily practices and do them for two weeks. At the end, you can renew or alter the practices.

FREESTYLE DEDICATION OF MERIT:
A DECLARATION OF INTERDEPENDENCE

Holding Truth as Selflessly Evident

All beings carry equal inheritance

Endowed by the stamp of consciousness

With unalienable longing

They rub inner genie lamps

Begging to be granted a unifying wish

To express neverlasting brilliance

Scalping front-row seats in reality's ampitheater

Hustling a niche

In a world that just shakes its head

When you ask it to please hold still

In a galaxy that laughs

When pundits spout singular causes
on bobble-brain talkshows

In a universe that may only be fathomed

By those who get the knock-knock joke
of trying to figure it out

That whenever this neverlasting connection is
misunderstood

The genie's lamp corrodes

An alchemy in reverse

The habit of isolation
seeks the syringe of dogma

Self becomes a prison

Other becomes the warden

The world becomes a post-cynical junkyard

Filled with the found objects
of apathy and fundamentalism

Yet the glimpse of connection never fades

It splashes rainbow-slicks across the cell

Leaving the grease-stain transparency

Of what lies beyond the wall

And when beings receive those glimpses

May they train in true alchemy

So that

Cynicism becomes intelligence

Consumerism becomes generosity

FREESTYLE DEDICATION OF MERIT

Entertainment becomes art

Detachment become energy

Marketing becomes invitation

And a glimpse becomes vision.

—ETHAN NICHTERN

BROOKLYN, 2007

ACKNOWLEDGMENTS
(A.K.A. HUGS IN INK)

TO JANICE RAGLAND AND DAVID NICHTERN for un-repayable generosity; Sakyong Mipham Rinpoche for being the baddest Buddhist teacher this side of the Himalayas (and also the kindest); Acharyas Arawana Hayashi, Dr. Gaylon Ferguson, and Eric Spiegel for showing me (and many others) how to deal with life over the years; Cyndi Lee for her care and support; Carol O'Donnell for convincing me I was a writer; Allen Ginsberg for convincing me that all writing is inherently poetry; Sarah Herrington for being Sarah Herrington; My whole family in the Northeast and down in Dixie, Dorothy Barangan, Nomi Kleinman, Juan Carlos Castro, Kyle Smith, Emily Herzlin and the WHOLE damn crew at The Interdependence Project (too many beautiful peeps to mention) for co-producing the ideas in this book AND for developing such a creative and hopeful community; President Richard Reoch and all the folks in the Shambhala community for their wisdom and decency; all the teachers and sangha at OM Yoga Center for practicing the interdependence of mind and body; Noah Levine and the Dharma Punx crew for demonstrating that tradition means nothing if it ain't relevant to who you are; Josh Bartok and Rod Meade Sperry at Wisdom Pubs for having their gentle fingers on the neo-dharmic pulse; Linda Loewenthal for being the best 007 secret agent; Kelly Notaras, Ellen Scordato, Abby Rasminsky, Greg Pierce, Crystal Gandrud, Eva Talmadge, Lisa Weinert, Cassie Peterson, and Sharifa Rhodes-Pitts for their many insights about this book; Jeff Zimbalist, Ian Koebner, Carissa Guild, Greg Zwahlen, Lodro Rinzler, Acharya Adam Lobel, Drew Buckland, Laura Luitje, Evan Rock, Matthew Steinfeld, Whitney Joiner, Ciprian Iancu, Jeff Grow, Alex Barocas, Doug McGowan, Eric Schneiderman, Susan Piver, Carol Hyman, Acharya Bill Mckeever, Elizabeth Josephson, Ishmael Beah, Frank Mauro, Joe Miller, Margi Young, and Sarah Trelease, each for eclectic modes of friendship, guidance, and so much creative inspiration, and to everyone else please accept a big hug the next time I see you because we gotta save some trees here . . . not to mention the planet!

ABOUT WISDOM

WISDOM PUBLICATIONS, a nonprofit publisher, is dedicated to making available authentic works relating to Buddhism for the benefit of all. We publish books by ancient and modern masters in all traditions of Buddhism, translations of important texts, and original scholarship. Additionally, we offer books that explore East-West themes unfolding as traditional Buddhism encounters our modern culture in all its aspects. Our titles are published with the appreciation of Buddhism as a living philosophy, and with the special commitment to preserve and transmit important works from Buddhism's many traditions.

To learn more about Wisdom, or to browse books online, visit our website at www.wisdompubs.org.

You may request a copy of our catalog online or by writing to this address:

Wisdom Publications
199 Elm Street
Somerville, Massachusetts 02144 USA
Telephone: 617-776-7416
Fax: 617-776-7841
Email: info@wisdompubs.org
www.wisdompubs.org

The Wisdom Trust

As a nonprofit publisher, Wisdom is dedicated to the publication of Dharma books for the benefit of all sentient beings and dependent upon the kindness and generosity of sponsors in order to do so. If you would like to make a donation to Wisdom, you may do so through our website or our Somerville office. If you would like to help sponsor the publication of a book, please write or email us at the address above.

Thank you.

Wisdom is a nonprofit, charitable 501(c)(3) organization affiliated with the Foundation for the Preservation of the Mahayana Tradition (FPMT).